Feeding Sense

A **sensible** approach to your baby's **nutrition and health**

Megan Faure, Katherine Megaw & Dr Simon Strachan

METZ PRESS

DEDICATION

To all the beautiful little patients we have seen over the years and will continue to see in practice; you, Dear Children, have taught us about everything. It is, after all, all about the children.

Published by Metz Press
1 Cameronians Avenue, Welgemoed 7530, South Africa

First edition 2010
Reprinted 2011, 2012
Copyright © Metz Press 2012
Copyright illustrations © Metz Press
Text copyright © Megan Faure, Katherine Megaw, Simon Strachan

Publisher & editor	Wilsia Metz
Proofreader	Francie Botes
Design & layout	Liezl Maree
Illustrations	Nikki Miles
Index	Wilsia Metz
Print production	Andrew de Kock
Printing and binding	Paarl Media, 15 Jan van Riebeeck Avenue, Paarl
ISBN	978-1-920268-70-1

Acknowledgements

There are few things as special as holding a new book in your hands. Like a parent holding their baby for the first time, as authors it brings us great joy to hold and deliver this book together.

Simon

"One of my life's ambitions was to write a book. Even though this is not a solo effort the elation and sense of achievement is fantastic. I offer great thanks to Kath and Meg for inviting me to join them in this project. Our collaboration of knowledge has been unselfish and inspiring."

Kath

"A special thank you to my co-authors: Meg Faure, who has walked this writing road before and whose invaluable experience and expertise brought the work of three authors together. Thank you to Dr Simon, a colleague and friend who was not only my children's paediatrician but also someone who inspired me 12 years ago to specialize in paediatric nutrition."

Meg

"Over many years I have watched Simon and Kath deliver uncomplicated, sense-able middle of the road nutrition and health advice to parents. Without hesitation I embarked on this journey with you. Thank you for being utterly professional and never losing sight of who the book was for – it is practically grounded in both your extensive work with babies."

Other professionals lead and guide us on our paths and we thank the doctors, therapists and other professionals with whom we work closely in order to help the little patients we see.

Thank you to the parents of these little ones we see, who want nothing more than to give their children the best as far as food and nutrition goes. Keep going – there is light at the end of your tunnels.

To our friends who have been a huge encouragement and support over the years. Thank you for always being willing to fetch and carry our children and for all the little extras. Thanks for your prayers and for being a listening ear to bounce off ideas and read and reread drafts.

Thank you to our publisher, Wilsia, for your patience, long hours and experience that fine tuned our work and brought this book together.

Kath

To my parents who many years ago gave me the gift of my career, thank you. To Karen and Jenna who have many years of babies ahead of them – I dedicate this book to the two of you and my future nieces and nephews. My beautiful children, Joshua, Teegan, Jaytn and our angel Sianne. You have each taught me so much in the field of feeding children, your patience as I work and help other mommies to feed their children is much appreciated. My Husband, Lionel, your encouragement, wisdom and support mean more than you can imagine. The way you love and care for our children and me is an inspiration and so appreciated.

Simon

Thank you to my children who help to motivate me and endure the hours of work at night. I love you all Tamsyn, Amy, Sarah, Musa, Adam and Rudi.

Meg

To my sister Lynne, to watch you feed your little boy while I wrote this book has reminded me about all the emotional and practical sides of feeding – thank you for sharing these with me. You are an incredible mother and to be part of your journey makes me immensely proud. My special husband Philip, I can do none of what I do without your time, love and support. Above all, you are the reason I can do what I do and still feel good about being a mom to our amazing children James, Alex and Em.

And to our God who has blessed us with every good gift – all glory and honour to Him.

Foreword

We are what we eat …

This short statement reflects the insight that food and eating have a profound influence not only on physical health but also on emotional and social functioning. On the one hand, food is the essential source of the basic nutrient building blocks of a healthy body, and the choice, composition and amount of food available to an individual may truly determine whether that individual grows normally or abnormally, becomes fat or thin or develops long-term risks of ill health or premature death. Food is a commodity with enormous political significance. It also has important psychological effects on behaviour and well-being.

On the other hand, eating is also an intensely social activity. At best, it engenders pleasure and mutual joy, but it can become a substitute activity for unmet emotional needs, and it can certainly arouse strong feelings of resentment, jealousy or conflict.

During infancy and early childhood all these issues take on added significance for both child and caregiver. The child is totally dependent for adequacy of feeding and the responsibility of making the right choices lies with the parent. What is the best feed, how often, how much is enough or too much, will baby be harmed or become allergic? Is breast-feeding really the best way of feeding baby and is it wrong to choose a formula?

Mothers want to do the right thing for their babies. Any difficulties with feeding while the child establishes its behavioural responses to its environment and its patterns of dietary likes and dislikes, can therefore be the cause of intense anxiety, stress and conflict. The dinner table can become a battle zone instead of a time of enjoyment and social learning. The child's weight gain or lack thereof may become the focus of guilt and despair.

Baby feeding is not only an emotionally laden subject; it is also big business. Not surprisingly therefore, mothers are bombarded with advertising claims to nutritional completeness or superiority of a bewildering array of commercially available options in baby formula, first foods, weaning foods, supplements or tonics. How on earth did grandma manage to feed her children? And for those with tight budgets, is there anything wrong in letting the infant eat the family's porridge rather than specially packed baby cereal?

I have enjoyed reading this book. The authors have selected common topics of baby feeding and nutrition and have provided both a factually grounded source of scientific information as well as answers to many nagging questions that mothers may not know whom to ask. They have used an easy-to-read informal style that converts professional advice into conversational information. I would like to believe that mothers using this book might feel more empowered to approach their doctor, nurse or dietician for clarification, or with further questions regarding their own situational problems.

After all, while nutrition is a science with reasonably established boundaries and parameters, baby and infant feeding is an interaction between two people and therefore a unique opportunity for a mutually satisfying relationship! This book should help cement this relationship with practically useful information.

DF Wittenberg MD FCP(SA)
Emeritus Professor, University of Pretoria

Contents

PROLOGUE

Within every mother is a deep-seated calling to feed her baby well. You may find that you measure your efficacy as a mom by whether or not your little one thrives nutritionally. When things go wrong and feeding is a challenge, you may experience high levels of anxiety and feel that you have failed. But your emotional relationship with your child is the priority in the first few years; therefore it is important not to let feeding become an area of high concern with negative feelings.

Feeding Sense offers you a sensible approach to feeding your baby and toddler. You will be guided through how to nourish your baby well at each age. Breast-feeding, bottle feeding and solids are three very different stages of feeding and problems can arise at any time.

You may find breast-feeding a synch, skip the bottle feeding stage and then find solids a real challenge. On the other hand, breast-feeding may be a real challenge for you, yet something you prioritise, and all you may need is some practical advice in order to breast-feed successfully. Other moms may have a baby who has serious feeding problems, such as a preemie or a baby with a cleft palate. This book is for all of you.

Feeding Sense provides solutions for each stage of feeding and practical guidance along the way in a gentle manner, with information backed by thorough research.

We suggest you read **Chapter 1** to get a sense of how to feed your baby holistically and what nutrition is important. Thereafter you may choose to read the entire **Section 1** or only the chapter relevant to your feeding challenge. **Section 2** is the age band chapters that will guide you through feeding your baby at each stage.

Nutrition – the pathway to health

Mary grew up in a home where meal times were sacred; her mom spent hours preparing wonderful meals. Now, as a granny, her mom is always dispensing advice on what food is good or bad for her grandchildren. This all adds to Mary's concerns and feelings of guilt. Her toddler is an atrocious eater; in fact, he exists on white bread and yogurt. Nothing green ever enters his mouth and at some meals not even his favourite foods are saved from the floor. As if this isn't enough, breast-feeding her second son, Max, was a nightmare. He would not latch and her milk had dwindled and now she is formula-hopping in an attempt to find a milk that will not constipate him. Mary feels desperate and dislikes this aspect of mothering. It is hard to imagine nourishing family dinners around a dinner table when she can't even feed her boys at this age.

The moment you conceived your precious little one, your mind probably shifted towards your diet and which nutrients you should be taking in. You probably had great expectations about how you would feed your newborn and may have invested in wonderful recipe books to entice your toddler to eat. This focus on nutrition is a valid one, as what goes into your baby will have an enormous impact on many areas of his development. But the effect on his development goes much further than simply a nutritious diet. The emotional, sensory and social aspects of feeding are largely overlooked but have just as significant an impact on your baby's health and development. As your baby's primary caregiver, you are the one who will help him establish good eating habits for the rest of his life. What a wonderful opportunity!

THE NUTRITION JOURNEY

Your baby's nutrition journey begins **in utero**. In the perfect womb world, your baby receives nutrition through the placenta. By six weeks' gestation, almost every substance you ingest (both healthy and dangerous) crosses the placenta and is absorbed by your growing baby. What you eat in pregnancy will directly impact your baby's intelligence, health and allergy profile for life. (Chapter 8 deals with healthy nutrition in pregnancy.)

In the last weeks of pregnancy, you will notice **colostrum** – a creamy white substance – being secreted in tiny quantities from your nipples. This 'first food' contains precious nutrients as well as antibodies from which your baby will benefit for life. (Chapter 2 on breast-feeding expands on the wonders of this first food.)

In the first four to six months of life, your baby will receive *all* his nutrition from **milk** – breast or formula. Breast milk is the perfect food for your baby and formulas are carefully designed to mimic breast milk as closely as possible. (Chapters 2 and 3 discuss milk feeds.)

Later, milk will become secondary to **solid** food (Chapter 4), which fulfils all your baby's nutritional needs as he approaches his first birthday. The first three years are a whirlwind journey that will set your child on course for healthy eating into adulthood.

THE IMPORTANCE OF SENSE-ABLE FEEDING

Deeply ingrained in each of us is the need to provide a nutritious diet and meet our growing baby's needs on a dietary level. There are good reasons for you to take this aspect of parenting very seriously. Balanced eating and a healthy diet in the formative years have immediate or short-term benefits as well as a profound long-term effect:

Benefits in the baby years

- A satisfied, well-fed baby is a more **settled baby**. If your baby is hungry he is more likely to be fractious.
- Your baby's **development** is a direct result of his diet – he needs sufficient energy and specific nutrients to learn from and explore his world.
- A hungry baby won't **sleep** well for long stretches.

Benefits in the school years

- **Attention span difficulties** and **hyperactivity** in childhood have been conclusively linked to alcohol consumption and drug abuse in pregnancy.
- **Intelligence** and **school achievement** are associated with a wholesome diet and critical nutrients provided during pregnancy and the early feeding period.
- **Allergies** frequently manifest in the short to medium term and early feeding can have a direct effect on this.

Benefits in adulthood

- **Healthy weight management** such as avoiding obesity and limiting eating disorders may be affected by the way you feed your baby in the early years.
- **Diabetes** can develop as a result of the types and amounts of sugars and highly processed food your baby has in infancy and childhood.
- Overall **health**, from liver function to the health of his heart, cholesterol levels and blood pressure, is affected by eating patterns instilled in the formative years.

THE FEEDING QUADRANT

Each meal – breast, bottle or plateful of food – carries not only nutrients, but love, sensory, social and emotional elements that feed and nourish your baby.

At birth, your baby has all the genetic potential to determine who he will be, in which areas he will excel, his health, predisposition to a particular disease and even allergies. But we also know that it is not just his **genes** that determine this. **Nurture**, which includes stimulation, providing a stable emotional base, food and so much more, is the way in which you impact on your baby's development.

Feeding is a very tangible part of parenting and a vital ingredient of giving your baby the best start in life. It is important to know that healthy feeding is multi-faceted – it is not simply *what* you feed your baby. *Feeding Sense* will change the way you think about this, covering not only the 'what to feed your baby' and 'when to feed what' but also the 'how' and why' and 'with what emotion'.

The feeding quadrant is a way of considering four elements present in each and every meal – four aspects of early feeding that will shape your baby's eating habits and health for life:

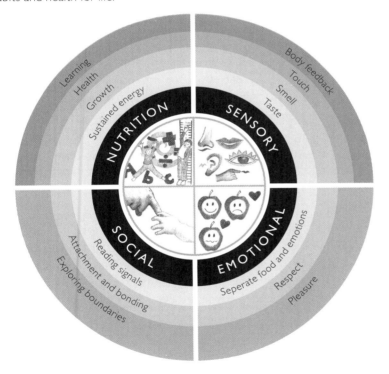

SENSE-ABLE FEEDING
From the first nutritious feed of colostrum to an inviting plate of finger food, each meal provides many different nutrients. Nutrients are the molecules in foods that the body uses to function correctly and stay healthy.

Nutrition

Everything you eat in pregnancy and each feed or meal you give your baby and toddler is digested into small particles that we call nutrients. Nutrients are the part of each meal that provides the building blocks for growth, development and your baby's future health. Nutrients provide:

SUSTAINED ENERGY

Your baby needs **energy** to live and interact in the world. Each second millions of activities requiring energy take place within your baby's body, such as building new cells as well as normal breathing, brain development and getting rid of toxic waste. The energy to perform these functions, as well as to sleep well, explore the world and interact, comes from food. Fats in food are one good source of energy. Another source of energy is foods that contain carbohydrates, which are digested or broken down in the gut into small particles that can be absorbed into the blood stream. These foods provide this energy to each individual cell in the form of glucose or blood sugar. In a nutshell, food is human fuel.

Food for energy	Breast or formula milk
	Wholegrain breads, cereals and porridge, pasta, rice
	Fats like avocado pear, olive oil, nuts and seeds

GROWTH

The first 12 months are the most dynamic period of **growth** for your baby. He will grow physically by increasing in length, head circumference and weight. His brain alone will double in weight in the first year. Foods that contain protein are broken down into amino acids which are the building blocks for every cell and function in your baby's body. Babies who do not receive the correct nutrition may show delays in growth and development. Food is critical for growth.

Food for physical growth	Breast or formula milk
	Dairy and soya
	Eggs, lean meats, chicken, fish, beans, lentils and nuts

HEALTH

Food plays a significant role in your baby's **immunity** – his body's defence against infection. A child's immune system develops and matures from the ninth week of pregnancy until the age of 14, which explains why young children are more susceptible to infections. Your baby's immune system needs to be nourished by essential micro nutrients to function efficiently. Nutrients and micro nutrients that bolster immunity include vitamins, minerals and even antibodies (found in breast milk only).

Food for immunity	Breast milk
	Whole grains
	Fruits and vegetables
	Lean meat, chicken and fish

LEARNING

The nutrients your baby receives *in utero* and from the day he is born, have a bearing on his intelligence and learning potential. His brain has the huge task of connecting the brain cells via synapses, which is vital for learning and physical development. These connections are coated in a sheath called myelin. This coating is vital for swift transmission of messages in the brain and is formed from essential fatty acids that are derived from foods high in fats.

Food for brain development	Breast milk and some formulas Oily fish, nuts and seeds

A balanced, age-appropriate diet will provide all the nutrients and micronutrients we need for health, growth, development and learning.

Sensory aspect of eating

The sensory aspect of feeding is a critical part of the eating experience. Sensory input tells your baby about the qualities of food, helps him to eat 'safe foods' and contributes to the pleasurable aspect of eating, which is essential. Your new baby is on a journey as he learns not only about the taste, smell and texture of food, but also starts to interpret his internal sensory messages.

TASTE

Taste is a protective sense designed to prevent us from eating toxic or dangerous substances. It senses pleasure, too, and has a direct impact on your baby's appetite – when food tastes good, he will want more of it. If a taste is unknown to your baby, he may not like it or take a while to develop a liking for it. If your baby is exposed to a wide variety of tastes, he is significantly less likely to be a fussy eater later. To a degree one's food preferences are *learnt through exposure*.

Your baby's tongue has millions of taste buds that sense the taste of a food and send a message to the brain. The brain decides if the food is good to eat and sends messages to the mouth and stomach to release saliva and other digestive juices that aid digestion.

SMELL

Smell is integrally linked with taste. As a flavour or smell enters your nose and mouth, it is dissolved and absorbed and sent to the brain. Unlike all other senses, smells do not pass through a relay centre in the brain (the thalamus) but go directly to the emotion and memory centre (the limbic system). This means that smells create memories and associations very quickly. Smells support appetite and assist in the release of saliva and other digestive juices. Surround your baby with smells conducive to feeding:

- Natural mommy smells (not strong perfumes) whilst breast-feeding.
- Lovely food aromas when offering solids.

SENSE-ABLE FEEDING
Expose your baby to a wide variety of flavours in the food you eat during pregnancy and breast-feeding and as soon as he is on solids – this will decrease the chance of picky eating later.

SENSE-ABLE FEEDING
If your baby is over-tired or oversensitive to smells, he may have difficulty eating in a environment such as the kitchen, where strong smells may be prevalent.

TOUCH

Feeding involves touch on the face and in the mouth. Touch will facilitate your newborn's feeding as he roots towards touch on the side of his face and begins to suck as the nipple touches his mouth. When eating solids, dealing with a variety of textures helps develop the muscles of your baby's cheeks and tongue, which is important for speech later. Exposure to such a variety also helps to limit fussy feeding.

FEEDBACK FROM THE BODY

Interoception is the body's internal message system. At the start of a feed, your baby may feel hunger or that his tummy is empty. Later in a feed or meal, his tummy will feel full. These feelings of hunger and fullness are communicated via interoception. Other information about his body, such as discomfort from acid reflux or a gas bubble in your baby's tummy is communicated in the same way. This is vital sensory information and you need to help your baby listen to the messages and learn to interpret them. This is the start of appetite regulation – your baby receives a message (of hunger or fullness), interprets that message and responds by eating or stopping a feed.

The social side of eating

Mary found mealtimes with her toddler fraught with food battles. He would push his food away and often threw the plate on the floor in anger if she forced a mouthful down. She was sure he did not know when he was full and was just being naughty. She felt she was caught up in only how much her toddler ate and that there was no chance of a pleasant family meal when her toddler was such a horror at mealtimes.

It may be hard to imagine the social side of eating when every meal is a battle, but eating can be a wonderful social activity. Human beings are the only animals that eat socially and we use this to connect with others. Like Mary, you may become so focused on ensuring that your baby has adequate nutrition that you forget about the social element of eating. Eating, like all social issues, has boundaries and norms. It should involve a relationship between you and your baby with enjoyment shared whilst relating to each other within these boundaries.

UNDERSTANDING YOUR BABY'S EATING SIGNALS

In the womb, your baby is fed without having to signal or interact at all. In the first three months of life – a period of high transition – your baby has to start communicating about being hungry. He does this by using sounds and body language to communicate his needs. Your responsibility is to watch for his signals, interpret what he is trying to say, and then to fulfil his need. When you meet his needs, your baby feels understood, comforted, safe, and secure. As he grows older your baby learns to understand how his body signals that he is hungry or full and to communicate this to you.

There are three steps to reading your baby's feeding signals:

- **Watch**: Take time to watch your baby. Don't be in a hurry. Sit down with him at mealtimes and focus on him as you would if you were having a social meal with your family.
- **Interpret**: When you notice a consistent signal around mealtimes, you will learn to respond appropriately.
  - Hunger: Rooting frantically (rooting when touched on the side of the cheek is a reflex in young babies); opening mouth at the sight of the nipple, teat or spoon; if your new baby is very hungry, crying may be a hunger signal.
  - Full, milk feeds: Stops sucking for a while; pulls off the teat or nipple; pushes tongue out towards teat/nipple whilst feeding; turns head away.
  - Full, mealtimes: Pushes food out of his mouth; closes his mouth (occasionally a new feeder will close his mouth until he has tasted the flavour of the food and then carry on feeding); turns away; pushes bowl or spoon away; stands up in high chair (which may also signal boredom when your baby may need to be diverted and then will remain seated for longer to eat the meal).
- **Respond**: After taking the time to interpret your baby's hunger or full signals, you must act consistently.
  - Offer a feed if hunger is indicated.
  - Engage with your baby with enjoyment while feeding him.
  - Respect your baby's full signal by not force-feeding him.
  - Reciprocate and talk back to your baby when you notice a signal, for example: "Yes, I know you are hungry" or "Oh, you are telling me you are full".

ATTACHMENT AND BONDING

Your relationship and the way you relate to your baby will start with the first feed and keep developing through into childhood meals. Your hormones and the close touch whilst breast-feeding will cause you to fall hopelessly in love with your baby. Likewise bottle-feeding is a bonding experience as you hold, cherish and nourish your little one with love. Soon, reading your baby's signals whilst he feeds and interpreting them accurately and with empathy adds another dimension to the bond that ties you.

EXPLORING BOUNDARIES

Your family will have social boundaries that may differ from those of other families – this is part of the social side of eating. Your baby will eventually explore boundaries at mealtimes. Healthy mealtime boundaries include eating at a certain place, at given times and with certain manners. Like other social norms, these boundaries are learnt over time. While you do not want to get into battles with your baby at mealtimes, you can gently introduce healthy habits through example and reinforce them with consistency.

While you do want to encourage table manners and boundaries around meals, bear the following in mind:

- How much your baby eats is **never** a boundary issue.
- Feeling and mashing food in his hands is a sensory exploratory process that all babies under the age of two years go through.
- Throwing utensils on the floor for you to pick up is part of learning object permanence between six and twelve months of age.
- Talking to and distracting your baby by playing with cars on the table, 'doing airplane', unpacking Dad's tool box or storytelling, is often part of social mealtimes – no one likes to eat in silence focussing only on the next mouthful. Talking to and interacting with your baby takes the focus off the task of eating.

Your baby's emotions and eating

On Friday evenings the family would gather and Mary would watch Sarah, her experienced sister-in-law – mother of three – feed her brood. Sarah's two older children would sit together at the table, one in a high-chair, and eat at the same time. She seemed to be able to read their signals so well and would tell stories and sing nursery rhymes. When Zachary, the toddler, was finished he would say "all done" and after offering one more mouthful, Sarah would tell him he could go and play. He was a skinny child but his mom respected his appetite and never seemed stressed if he ate too little. Mary was at a complete loss, she found it really hard to feed her toddler and was critical that her sister used distraction at mealtimes. But if she was honest with herself it seemed to be a less stressful road to take.

We have seen how feeding your baby is an interactive process that is related to how you and your baby respond to each other. A positive feeding relationship is essential for your baby's long-term proper nutrition and growth. In addition, interactions related to feeding have a powerful impact on how your baby will feel about himself and the world in the long term. Eating not only provides nutrition and sensory and social experiences, it also brings with it an emotional energy.

It is very easy, like Mary, to allow mealtimes to be overshadowed by frustration and irritation while trying to feed your toddler. In truth almost every parent will admit to these feelings at mealtimes. But compare this to the more laid-back approach Sarah used – even though her toddler was small, she did not let mealtimes become a negative experience. We know that getting into food battles and allowing mealtimes to become stressful is very easy and is the trap almost every parent will fall into, but it is worth keeping a relaxed and positive emotional tone at mealtimes as you feed your baby.

SEPARATE FOOD AND EMOTIONS

Just as emotions release chemical messages in the brain, so does food. We talk about comfort eating because some foods, such as chocolate and pasta, release feel-good chemicals in the brain. It poses a risk to your baby's long-term weight management if he learns to rely on food for comfort instead of relationships and internal strategies to meet these needs.

All babies and toddlers cry and yell and have temper tantrums – this is part of growing up. It is tempting to discourage emotional outbursts or to offer a feed or food to calm your baby or toddler. If an outburst is not related to hunger, but is because your little one feels sad, angry or frustrated, it is important that you do not offer food as solace. Instead of giving your child something to eat as comfort, rather offer a hug or some positive attention, such as reading to him, or a sleep if needed. If the only way you respond to your baby's cries is by feeding, he will learn that discomfort or emotional distress needs to be satisfied with food.

> **SENSE-ABLE FEEDING**
> When your baby is hungry, feed him. When he is crying for another reason, such as tiredness, overstimulation or discomfort, address that need. Take time to establish if the cry is hunger or if there is an emotional reason for his behaviour.

RESPECT

Feeding often becomes a food battle because of parents' expectations. It is easy to fall into the trap of setting yourself and your baby eating goals based on a growth chart, a recommended daily intake or the eating pattern of your friend's baby. To avoid food battles you need to establish who is responsible for what at mealtimes. As parent/caregiver, you are responsible for:

- Where the meal will be eaten (see page 148).
- What is being offered. Set your baby up for success, not failure, by offering food he enjoys and is most likely to eat. If you are introducing a new food or food that he has refused before, offer it with something he likes.
- When the feed will take place. If your body consistently gets breakfast at a certain time each day it will create an appetite at around that time each day. Of course with little ones you do need a degree of flexibility and if your baby is hungry a little earlier than you planned, don't be rigid.

Your baby is responsible for how much. He will over time learn to read his full signals. Identify and respect your baby's signals; he hasn't read 'the books' or the directions on the formula tin. He simply knows fullness, hunger and how you respond to his signals. In leaving this aspect to your baby, bear in mind the following:

- He is an **individual** with his own personality and temperament and appetite.
- Some **days** your baby will eat and drink all the milk and food you planned for the day and other days he may eat less than half.
- His appetite can easily be **disrupted** by illness, teething, him being overtired or simply a new environment, especially if he is a very sensitive baby.

When you are feeling frustrated or upset with how little your baby has eaten, you communicate through non-verbal signals such as touch, eye contact, body language, facial expression, space or distance, without actually saying a word.

Experiencing these emotions is not wrong, but it is helpful to recognize negative emotions that may spoil the pleasure of eating for you and your baby. If feeding your baby is frustrating, find someone you can chat to, be it your mom, sister, friend or someone in the medical profession that can lend a listening ear and reassure you. After all, you are the best parent for your baby, no matter how you may feel on some days!

PLEASURE

As adults we derive **pleasure** from food and eating. We must not forget that the same should and will be true for our babies and children. It is easy to be so focused on eating for growth, health, immunity and sleep that we forget that enjoyment is important too. Research has shown that when the eating experience is pleasurable, babies and children will consume more food and more nutritional food. A pleasurable eating experience should be one of the foremost goals in your mind when feeding your baby.

LET GO

Let go and enjoy feeding your baby

- View the journey of feeding your baby as an exciting adventure.
- Do not focus on gourmet meals and interesting flavours at this stage – variety of menu and culinary delights will come later. If you put too much emphasis on the menu and invest too much energy on the novelty, you will be frustrated when your toddler upends his bowl.
- If your baby refuses a certain food, offer another option and don't sweat the bowl of food you will need to throw away. Offer the offending food at another time.
- Don't get caught up in quantities – babies can obtain most of the nutrients they need in 24 hours from much less than you would think. Appetites vary extensively too and some days your baby will eat more than others.
- Let go – allow your older baby (from eight months onwards) control and give him the opportunity to self-feed. Have two bowls – one for you to spoon feed from and one for him to explore from.

Mealtimes are a special time – you get to mould a little person's feeding habits and relationship with food that will set them up for life. Healthy, nutritious food nurtures and sustains health, but developing a healthy attitude to food and mealtimes is just as important.

We will guide you through this journey so that you can have fun while making some very important decisions about your baby's nutrition.

CHAPTER 2

Breast-feeding

Becoming a mother was something Anna had dreamed about her entire life. She had an amazing delivery and fell in love the instant she set eyes on Sarah. Her little cap of dark hair and the smell of her newborn space filled Anna with delight each time she held her precious bundle. But Anna came to dread feed times. She had expected breast-feeding to come naturally and to feed for a year, just as she had been. But her body had other ideas: breast-feeding was so difficult. By day three, her nipples were a bleeding mess and her breasts engorged with milk. She thought it could get no worse but two weeks down the line she got mastitis. She was not the only one battling; her closest friend from antenatal classes was also struggling, with the added stress of too little milk. As the friends poured out their breast-feeding woes over a cup of tea, it crossed their minds that they should have been better prepared for breast-feeding than the birth. The delivery was over in 12 hours but breast-feeding goes on for months – well hopefully, if they didn't give up!

There is no doubt that breast-feeding is one of the most emotionally charged aspects of early parenting. Like many women you may have set out to breast-feed only to find this a challenging part of mothering. You may have unrealistic expectations of what it will feel like to breast-feed and how easily it will come. It is often an area in which advice is conflicting and criticism is rife. When breast-feeding goes well, it fills mothers with delight and a feeling of success, but when things go wrong, despair and guilt may be the overriding emotion.

WHY IT MAY BE DIFFICULT

It is undisputed that breast milk is the best nutrition for your baby in the first few months. The World Health Organisation recommends exclusive breast-feeding until at least six months of age. Formula milk companies are not allowed to advertise to attract moms to formula milk. Most women set out to breast-feed for as long a possible. So with the intense focus from all quarters on breast-feeding, why is it that even with the best intentions so many moms are not successful and make the decision to bottle feed within a short time? There are a multitude of reasons why you may battle with breast-feeding:

- In all likelihood, you did have not have the benefit of watching your mom or sister breast-feed at close proximity, so this skill has not been passed on as naturally as it was for previous generations and in cultures where communal parenting is more common.
- There is little or no focus on the teaching of breast-feeding technique ahead of the birth of your baby.

- Advice on feeding routines is conflicting; the advice to get your baby into a rigid routine in the early weeks is not conducive to establishing your milk supply.
- Breasts are not calibrated so even if you have established a good supply, when your baby is crying you may wonder if you have sufficient milk.

With sensible guidance and perseverance you can expect breast-feeding to be a positive experience and you may well be able to breast-feed for as long as you aim to.

REASONS TO BREAST-FEED

Breast milk is the gold standard against which all formulas are measured for good reason, and breast-feeding has many advantages:
- Breast milk is the most complete form of nutrition for young babies. Your breast milk has just the right amount of fat, energy, water, and protein required for your baby's growth and development. For most babies breast milk is easier to digest than other alternatives.
- Breast milk is the only milk that contains antibodies, which help to build your baby's immune system. Breast-fed babies are better equipped to fight off infections and disease and are sick less often.
- Exclusive breast-feeding for the first four months of life may also protect your child against allergies, especially allergic skin conditions like eczema.
- Breast-feeding also has many benefits for moms. It uses up some fat stores and helps you get back into your jeans. It also helps your uterus to return to its original size a lot sooner and reduces the risk of breast and ovarian cancers.
- On a more practical level, breast-feeding is convenient, it saves time and money. It is always available, at the right temperature and in a sterile 'container'.

What is important is that even if you are able to breast-feed for only a short period of time, your baby will benefit in numerous ways from breast milk.

| HIV AND BREAST-FEEDING | If you are HIV positive, breast-feeding in combination with formula feeds increases the risk of transmitting HIV to your child. If you can breast-feed **exclusively** and are taking antiretroviral medication there is evidence that the benefits of the antibodies in breast milk outweigh the risks of transmitting the virus. If you are not taking antiretroviral medication, your baby must take antiretrovirals the entire time that you are breast-feeding. Once formula is introduced, stop breast-feeding altogether. |

BREAST MILK BASICS

Breast milk does not always look the same because it changes composition during a feed, as well as throughout the day. In comparison with full-cream cow's milk, breast milk appears thin and watery, and may have a blue or yellow tint to it. It can even take on a tinge of green, orange or another colour depending on what you have been eating. Occasionally milk may take on a pink colour as a result of a small amount of blood from your nipples, but this does not spoil the milk at all.

When expressed and stored in a refrigerator, breast milk separates. Sometimes there is a thick layer of cream or fat on top, other times a thin layer. Sometimes the milk looks lumpy, and sometimes it can be nearly clear towards the bottom of the container. All of this is completely normal and does not mean the milk has soured. Soured milk has a distinct smell.

Breast milk is a fully comprehensive meal in liquid form. It is made up of many components.

Fat

If you were to remove all the water from breast milk, just over half of what is left (55%) is fat, including a high level of cholesterol. These fats and cholesterol are vital because babies, toddlers and young children need high levels of fats for the development of the nervous system. These essential fats are required to cover and protect nerve cells and are a crucial component of brain development.

Carbohydrates

Carbohydrates make up about 37% of breast milk. While we often think of carbohydrates as bread, pasta and rice, in actual fact all sugars are carbohydrates. In breast milk, most of the carbohydrates are in the form of lactose, which is milk sugar. Lactose provides your baby with energy so that she can do the things that babies do: breathe, eat, cry, wriggle, pass stools, learn, grow and develop.

Proteins

Breast milk contains 8% protein, which is essential for your baby's growth. Colostrum is particularly high in protein to stabilize your newborn's blood sugar, whereas mature milk has a slightly lower but consistent level of protein (1 g per 100 ml). As your baby grows her protein needs increase. Therefore, by six months of age she will need protein from sources other than milk, in other words from solid foods.

Vitamins, minerals, and more

Breast milk contains vitamins and minerals which the manufacturers of formulas attempt to simulate. However, there are over 100 different nutritional components in breast milk, all of which contribute to your baby's health as she grows.

Probiotics are healthy microorganisms that contribute to a healthy digestive system by maintaining the balance between healthy and harmful bacteria in the digestive tract. Breast milk does not contain probiotics but contains high doses of lactose which, when fermented, encourages the growth of probiotics. Since probiotics are so important for preventing the unhealthy bacteria from taking over, breast milk plays an important role in keeping your baby's gut healthy.

SMART FOOD

Breast milk is amazing simply because it can change in composition depending on your baby's needs.

We only make one kind of milk (full cream), but the fat molecules in the milk stick to each other and the inside of the milk ducts, so the first milk comes out without the fatty molecules. The letdown reflex helps to force the fat molecules along the ducts and as your baby feeds, more and more fat molecules become available in the milk. The emptier your breast feels, the higher the fat content of the milk. Avoid switching to the second breast too soon.

Over a period of months your breast milk changes according to your growing baby's needs:

SENSE-ABLE FEEDING
Your breast milk at birth of a full-term baby is perfectly suited to the needs of your newborn baby, and at four months, perfectly suited for your four-month-old.

- Colostrum is made during the last few weeks of pregnancy and the first week after birth. It has three times more protein but less sugar, and less fat than mature milk. In addition, this magic early milk is full of antibodies which provide your baby with immunity to fight germs and bacteria. Your baby didn't have to fight germs when she was in your womb, but once out of the womb, it is important that she receives antibodies since her own immune system has not developed yet.
- Mature milk continues to change over the course of the first year. As your baby grows, breast milk alone will no longer adequately meet her changing nutritional needs and you should introduce solids between four and six months of age.

BREAST-FEEDING IS A SENSORY EXPERIENCE

The sensory system is the foundation of motor as well as emotional development. At every moment and in every interaction, your baby is taking in sensory information from her environment. Being breast-fed is the closest your baby gets to being in the womb again on a sensory level. It is a precious experience not just for the nutrients it delivers but developmentally too.

Taste

The flavour of breast milk changes with every feed. At all times, being made up of lactose (milk sugars) your breast milk is sweet, which your baby is primed to prefer. In addition to this underlying sweetness, your breast milk carries the flavours of what you last ate. Garlic, onions, curries and other robust flavours are strongly transferred in breast milk. Babies who are exposed to a wide range of flavours in breast milk in these early days are more open to eating a wide range of foods when solids are introduced.

Touch

Breast-feeding is one of the most sensual touch experiences you will have with your baby. Only bathing with your baby and kangaroo care (skin to skin on your chest) will come as close to this experience on a tactile level. Your baby feels skin to skin touch on her hands, face and within her mouth. In addition, her entire body feels your body and the touch of your hands as you hold her. Your baby's touch receptors on her face and within her mouth are more prolific than anywhere else on her body. These receptors are essential for survival as she roots towards your nipple when her cheek is touched near her mouth and as she conforms her mouth to your nipple. The suck reflex is elicited by pressure on her tongue and the roof of her mouth. Touch therefore also plays an important practical part in breast-feeding.

Smell

Held against your body, your baby takes in your body smell, which is comforting as it takes her back to the womb world. Do not use strong perfumes and deodorants as these mask your mommy smell and may be overpowering for your little one's strong sense of smell. Smell is integrally linked to appetite for all of us and so your baby will feed best with the smell of milk and mommy rather than overwhelming chemical odours. Preferably wash your clothes in neutral-smelling detergents and use a light deodorant.

Sight

At the moment of birth your baby can see clearly at a distance of 20 cm – the perfect distance from your nipple to your face. As she feeds, she sees your eyes, and the outline of your mouth and face with clarity.

Hearing

Held closely in your arms your baby hears your gentle murmurs as you encourage her to drink, she is familiar with your heartbeat and your voice both of which she heard *in utero*.

Position sense

The vestibular system registers that the reclining position for breast-feeding is different from being upright. Within weeks your baby will recognise this as her feeding position and begin to root for the nipple and prepare to feed. You will notice her pre-feeding sounds and as she looks for her food source when laid on her side against your body.

> **SENSE-ABLE FEEDING**
> Whole-body tactile experience is soothing for most babies and communicates love and paves the way for positive touch experiences later on.

PREPARING TO BREAST-FEED

Anna was conscious of eating all the right food for breast-feeding but had been warned to exclude so many foods to keep her baby from being colicky and developing allergies. As with all areas of parenting, there was a lot of conflicting advice on offer.

Eating whilst breast-feeding is not rocket science – you simply need to eat a well-balanced diet and drink enough liquids.

Fluid intake

You may be unusually thirsty during the first few days after birth as your body sheds excess fluid accumulated during pregnancy. Drink plenty of liquids, such as Rooibos tea, water, milk, and soup to quench your thirst. Liquids can be in any form, but be sure to limit your intake of caffeine. It is not necessary to force fluids beyond your thirst, but it is a good idea to drink something when you feel thirsty. Whenever you sit down to breast-feed, grab a glass of water or jungle juice to drink.

Food for energy

SENSE-ABLE FEEDING
Grab a healthy snack to eat while breast-feeding or keep wrapped snacks near your favourite breast-feeding spot.

Eat a wide variety of foods to get the calories, vitamins, and minerals you need to remain healthy. The best guide as to how much to eat should be your appetite. In general, mothers are hungrier during the first few months of breast-feeding, and you should not ignore feelings of hunger when producing milk for your baby. However, you do not need to eat for two – adding only an extra 500 calories per day is sufficient. (This is the equivalent of a peanut butter sandwich, an apple and a glass of milk.) Foods from the following food categories offer the most nutritional value:

RECOMMENDED DIET FOR A BREAST-FEEDING MOM

Food	Portion size	Number of portions per day
Chicken, fish, lean meat, beans, egg	Piece of meat or fish the size of your palm and the thickness of your hand ½ cup beans 1 egg	5 portions
Milk, cheese	250 ml milk 1 matchbox-size piece of cheese 250 ml yogurt	2 portions
Vegetables and fruit	Especially leafy green vegetables 1 cup raw/½ cup cooked 1 whole fruit	5 portions

Food	Portion size	Number of portions per day
Wholegrain breads, cereals, pasta and rice	1 slice bread ½ cup cooked pasta ½ cup cereal ⅓ cup rice	6 portions
Healthy fats and oils	¼ avocado pear 5 ml olive, canola or flaxseed oil 8 nuts	6 portions

Essential fatty acids

Omega 6 and Omega 3 are considered to be essential fatty acids (EFAs) and are vital for your baby's growth – particularly her brain development. If you are breast-feeding you should include natural sources of Omega 3 in your diet:

- Cold-water or oily fish and fish oils (salmon, mackerel, herring, tuna, sardines, anchovies); fresh fish is preferable
- Green leaves of vegetables
- Some seeds and nuts (flaxseeds, walnuts, canola, linseeds, pumpkin seeds)
- Some legumes (soy beans, kidney beans, haricot beans)

Multivitamin supplements

A good prenatal supplement will contain the essential vitamins and minerals you need during breast-feeding. It is important to continue taking this for the duration of breast-feeding. The supplement will include but won't be limited to:

- Calcium, which is essential for your baby's bones and teeth: 1 200 mg/day
- Zinc, which is essential for your baby's immune system: 12 mg/day
- Folic acid, which is essential for building protein tissue: 500 ug/day
- Iron, which is essential for carrying oxygen to the cells: 10 mg/day

Obviously you will avoid any food to which you are allergic while breast-feeding your baby. However, recent research shows that a breast-feeding mom must not avoid high-risk allergy foods like nuts, eggs, fish, wheat, dairy and soya unless she herself is allergic to that particular food. It has been suggested that exposing your baby to these high-risk foods via breast milk during breast-feeding may actually help your baby tolerate them at a later stage.

SENSE-ABLE FEEDING
Although getting rid of any extra weight gained during pregnancy may be a concern, strict weight-loss programmes are not recommended, especially during the first few months of breast-feeding.

HIGH-RISK ALLERGY FOODS

Other dietary considerations while breast-feeding

Spicy or gas-producing foods are common in the diets of many cultures, and these kinds of foods do not bother most babies. A few babies will develop gas or act colicky when their mothers eat certain foods. However, there are no specific foods that create problems for all babies. Unless you notice within six hours that your baby reacts every time you eat a particular food, there is no need to avoid it. Give it time as the more your baby is exposed to the food, the quicker she will get used to it.

The milk of *vegetarian moms* is usually as nutritionally appropriate as that of other mothers. Ensure that your diet contains adequate proteins by eating a wide variety of foods. Even if you are eating eggs and dairy products, you may require supplementary vitamin D, iron and calcium while breast-feeding. If you are a *vegan*, your milk may be deficient in vitamin B12 and you will need supplements.

Consumption of *alcohol* can negatively affect your baby's development. (See page 97 on foetal alcohol syndrome.) In addition, it can interfere with milk let-down (milk-ejection reflex), which may come as a surprise if you've been told an alcoholic beverage will enhance milk letdown by helping you feel more relaxed. Perhaps the most important point is that alcohol consumption can affect your ability to properly care for your baby. Alcohol has been conclusively linked to cot deaths when mothers sleep in the same bed as their baby after drinking.

<table>
<tr>
<td>EMOTIONAL AND PHYSICAL PREPARATION FOR BREAST-FEEDING</td>
<td>

- **Expect** breast-feeding to take a while to establish and to be quite time consuming in the early days. Your baby needs to feed on cue in the first two to six weeks. You may well have an easy time establishing your milk supply but your road to successful feeding will be smoother if you are happy to put in time and effort in the early days. Your milk supply should be established once your baby is six weeks old. Some pattern will have developed, creating a flexible routine.
- Your **nipples** will need to adapt to feeding and they will toughen up over time. By and large the only real damage to your nipples will be due to poor latching, so focus on getting this right. Do not heed any advice that encourages you to 'toughen up' your nipples with abrasive techniques. This will only make them more sensitive and likely to crack.
- If you can take the time to **watch** another mom latch her baby and breast-feed before you embark on the journey of feeding your baby, you may find that it comes a little more naturally.

</td>
</tr>
</table>

THE RIGHT START

The foundation for successful, sustainable breast-feeding is laid within hours of your baby's birth.

On day one

SENSE-ABLE FEEDING
In a normal, unmedicated birth, a baby placed on her mother's bare chest very soon after birth will 'crawl' up to the breast and latch on her own, such is her natural instinct to breast-feed at birth.

The sooner your baby goes to the breast after birth, the easier it will be for her to latch and suck effectively. Make sure your baby has unlimited access to your breast within four hours of birth. Keep her skin to skin, wearing only a nappy, between your breasts between feeds.

The way your baby is positioned and latched onto your breast will determine how comfortable you both feel and how easy or difficult it is for your baby to feed effectively. The frequent and effective draining of your breasts will also enable you to establish an adequate milk supply.

Helping your baby latch well

Whilst some moms do experience discomfort or even pain in the early days of breast-feeding, severe shooting pain is not normal and is usually associated with a poor latch. A good latch is important for comfort, good flow of milk, establishing a milk supply and to prevent nipple damage:

- Bring your baby to your breast – not your breast to your baby.
- Your baby's mouth should be wide open and both lips curled back.
- Your baby's chin will be tucked into your breast.
- Almost your entire areola (the dark area around your nipple) will be in her mouth, not just the nipple. You may see more areola above your baby's top lip than below her bottom lip.
- Your baby's tongue will be under the areola and over her lower gum.
- She has space to breathe. Tuck her bum in closer and/or move her across your body a little more.

SENSE-ABLE FEEDING
Latching properly is a corner-stone of problem-free breast-feeding.

Good latch

FEEDING POSITIONS

Sitting – cross-cradle hold

Sit comfortably in your bed or in a chair with your feet on the floor. Sit back with a feeding pillow on your lap. This position works very well for newborns in particular. Hold your baby in the opposite arm to the breast you will feed from, with your hand in a V-shape behind her neck and shoulders. Your baby's arms will be on either side of your breast, and her body tucked right into your body. Use your free hand to shape your breast initially, and then to support your other arm.

Football hold

This position is great if you have had a Caeser. Place your baby on a soft pillow with her legs under your arm and her head towards your breast. Her body will be lying in the waistline of your body. Bring her head up to your breast. You can use this position for the first few days and then switch to cross-cradle hold.

Lying

This position is great for a well-established breast-feeder once your baby has learnt how to latch on properly. It is very comfortable and relaxing. Lie on your side with your head on a pillow. Lie your baby next to you, tummy to tummy. Feed from your lower breast.

Position to slow down flow

At times you may find your baby struggles with the speed of your milk flow. Lie on your back with your head and shoulders lifted at a 45 degree angle, supported with a pillow or two. Place your baby on your body and help her to drink from your breast by supporting her head and shoulders. She will be drinking against gravity to slow down the flow of milk.

SENSE-ABLE FEEDING
Experiment with feeding positions until you find one that works well for you and your baby.

Feeding twins

You can choose to feed twins one at a time using any of the above positions or you can feed them together. The best position for feeding twins at the same time is to use the football hold on both sides. You could also feed one baby in a football hold and one in a sitting position. Both options are feasible.

ESTABLISHING A GOOD MILK SUPPLY

Milk supply is essential for successful breast-feeding, and how you go about the early days and weeks of breast-feeding are critical to establishing a good milk supply.

Feed on cue

Breast-feeding on cue means feeding your baby whenever she is hungry or shows signs of needing a feed. Babies don't eat out of boredom or habit; they eat when they need to. In the early days of breast-feeding, feeding on cue helps establish your milk supply. In addition, it encourages you to be baby focused, which is important for breast-feeding success. The secret is to know when your baby is hungry.

- In the first two weeks, if your baby cries, don't look at the clock to try to gauge whether she should be hungry. Rather feed her.
- Between two and six weeks, feed your baby if she is crying and more than two hours have passed since the last feed. Crying less than one hour since the last feed began is more likely to be due to tiredness, overstimulation or feeling too full.
- After about six weeks you may want to get into a more structured feeding programme. The choice is entirely yours and will depend on your circumstances: whether this is your first or second child; whether you need to go back to work at four months; whether you have additional help in the home and so on. Both on-cue and scheduled feeding have advantages and disadvantages and, if you understand them, you can make an informed decision on what will work best for you, your baby and your household.

	Feeding on cue	Scheduled feeding
Advantages	Establishes milk supply in the critical first six weeks. You encourage your baby to be an intuitive eater. Your baby's nutritionally changing needs will be easily met.	You can arrange to go out as you know when your baby is more likely to feed.
Disadvantages	You need to be with your baby at feed times. Your baby will feed more frequently. Sleep can be more disrupted for longer. The breast may become the sole pacifier and not only used for hunger.	Difficult to establish adequate milk supply in the early weeks. You might not be sensitive to frequency days when your baby will feed more often.

BREAST-FEEDING CHALLENGES

Breast-feeding, while not always easily established, is well worth working at. Not only is breast milk the best nutrition for your baby, it may well be a truly wonderful experience for you both.

Most of the challenges breast-feeding brings are dealt with in the age-related chapters in the second part of the book. However, there are common issues that may arise at any time on your breast-feeding journey.

Learning a new skill

The more support you have to establish breast-feeding, the better chance that you will have a positive experience. Here are some tips to grow your support network:
- Read about breast-feeding and seek advice, even before your baby is born.
- Speak to others who have breast-fed their babies and try to watch a mom breast-feed and latch her baby, even before your little one is born.
- Share information with your partner – it is very helpful to have a supportive partner.
- Ask your hospital for a name of a qualified lactation consultant who can assist you after birth.
- While you are learning to breast-feed, do so in the privacy of your own space until your confidence grows.
- Join a breast-feeding support group – don't be scared to ask for help.
- Write down your questions or concerns in a diary.
- Ask your questions again if you are still not sure.
- Be careful of information overload – choose two voices you trust and filter out all other advice.

Uncertainty over milk supply

Your baby is getting enough milk if
- She has six to eight wet nappies in 24 hours
- She is alert and responsive
- Her eyes are bright, lips moist and skin tone good
- She is gaining weight according to a *breast-feeding* growth chart.
- Her urine is pale in colour and odourless and her bowel actions vary in colour from green (occasionally) to mostly gold to yellow. In the first four to six weeks a breast-fed baby should have at least three loose yellow stools daily. Thereafter she can have anything from seven stools in one day to one stool in seven days.

Your milk supply will vary depending on the age and development of your baby, the number of feeds she is having and other factors, including your physical and emotional state. It is normal to go through stages of thinking that you are not producing enough milk for your baby. Rest assured that you will be wrong most of the time. Some reasons why you may feel you are not producing enough milk:
- **Your baby's weight gain slows down**
  Observe your baby's weight gain over a few weeks and not one or two weigh-ins. The average weekly weight gain changes as your baby grows during the

first year, starting at about 200 g and ending at about 50 g per week. There may be times when she gains more weight than anticipated and others when she gains less weight – this is normal.

- **Your baby is sucking her fist**
  This is a self-soothing strategy that develops at around nine weeks of age, not always a sign of hunger. Most babies explore their hands with their mouths and use them to self-calm. While it may be a hunger signal, do not read it as an indication that she wants more food every time she sucks her fists.
- **You do not feel a letdown reflex**
  The intensity of this sensation diminishes in some women after six to eight weeks and is not indicative of milk supply.
- **Your baby pulls on and off the breast**
  As your baby grows and develops she may suck for comfort and pull on and off the breast once she is satisfied by the milk, but re-attach for comfort. If your baby gets distracted once she is older, you may need to feed her in a less stimulating environment.
- **Your baby is unsettled**
  A baby who is overtired or overstimulated, or a sick baby will be unsettled and her fractiousness may or may not be hunger related.
- **Your breast milk looks thin**
  Breast milk is highly nutritious and satisfying despite its watery appearance when compared to infant formula or cow's milk.
- **Your baby feeds for a shorter time**
  As your baby becomes stronger she becomes more effective at draining your breast milk and can take in all the nutrition she needs within a few minutes.
- **You cannot express much milk**
  Babies have far more expertise at draining your breasts than a breast pump, so you may be an excellent source of milk but not the best expresser.
- **Your breasts become softer and smaller and stop leaking**
  Once breast-feeding is established you may find that the supply and demand cycle is working efficiently, so you no longer have excess milk leaking.
- **Your baby fusses at the breast and wants to feed more frequently**
  During a growth spurt, also known as frequency days, your baby will be hungrier and want to feed more. It is important to feed your baby according to the increased demand in order to increase your supply. Your body will soon catch up and you will be able to settle into a flexible routine again.

Low milk supply

Of course there is a chance that your concerns of low milk supply are valid, especially if:

- Your baby is poorly positioned on the breast
- Your baby has a poor sucking technique
- Your baby is not stimulating the breast sufficiently
- You have had breast surgery

- You are on oral contraceptives
- You are taking medication such as antihistamines and decongestants
- You have heightened anxiety
- You are suffering from depression
- You have been separated from your baby for prolonged periods.

If you are concerned that your baby is not thriving on your milk supply, seek advice from your healthcare professional and don't try and fix it alone. In the meantime, there are ways to increase your milk supply:

- Get lots of rest
- Eat a nutritious diet
- Drink sufficient liquid
- Limit intake of caffeine, alcohol and smoking
- Check your positioning and the sucking efficiency of your baby
- Stimulate your letdown reflex by providing warmth to your breast prior to feeding
- Offer an adequate number of feeds in 24 hours.

> **SENSE-ABLE FEEDING**
> Remove stimulating elements from the feeding environment if you find that your baby becomes distracted.

CHAPTER 3

Bottle feeding

After six gruelling weeks of breast-feeding, Marisa had finally thrown in the towel. She did not set out with any expectations about breast-feeding; in fact, she gave it little thought at all, assuming it would come naturally. She was surprised when it turned out to be such a challenge and she was faced with a switch to bottle feeding. She was even more surprised at her swinging emotions: distress as she faced 'giving up', guilt that she would not be doing the 'best' for her baby and then finally relief when she made the decision and moved ahead to a new method of feeding. She was also astounded to find out just how little advice and information there was out there for new mothers on bottle feeding and formulas. It seemed that in an attempt to encourage breast-feeding, the outside world simply avoided the subject of bottle feeding altogether.

SENSE-ABLE FEEDING
The decision to breast-feed or formula feed your baby is a very personal one.

While breast milk is the best food for your baby and your breasts are perfectly designed to produce milk, there may come a time sooner or later when bottle feeding (either expressed breast milk or formula milk) becomes your preferred method of feeding.

REASONS YOU MAY CHOOSE TO BOTTLE FEED

You may decide to introduce bottles to feed your baby either breast or formula milk for one of the following reasons:

- As an alternate method to feed your baby **expressed breast milk** as you are returning to work or need to have some freedom to be absent for the odd feed.
- To give your baby a **top-up feed** of expressed breast milk or formula if he is not gaining weight optimally.
- As a completely alternative feeding method because you cannot feed your baby – for a **medical reason** such as fear of passing on HIV or AIDS, or those that involve chemotherapy or treatment with certain medications that may make breast-feeding unsafe. You should check with your doctor or a lactation consultant if you are unsure if you should breast-feed with a specific condition. Note that recent research has shown that the benefits to your baby of exclusive breast-feeding outweigh the risks of transferring HIV to him (see page 20).
- **Breast surgery** such as a reduction may change your breast tissue, resulting in poor milk supply if your milk ducts have been severed. If this is the case, talk to your doctor about your concerns and work with a lactation specialist.
- You or your baby had a very **traumatic** time in the early days, for instance if you were very ill after the birth of your baby or if he was born very premature and cannot breast-feed initially.

- Your baby was not thriving on your breast milk and feeding had become a difficult and **stressful** aspect of parenting for you as you tried every method to build up your milk supply or cope with discomfort or repeated infections.
- If bottle-feeding is simply the way you **choose** to feed your baby.

Taking the decision to bottle feed will be the right choice for you and your baby if thought through carefully and on advice of a medical professional. When it comes to parenting you are the only expert on your baby and although you should heed advice, ultimately the choice that makes you feel most comfortable and relaxed is the right choice for you and your baby. Feeding your full-term baby expressed breast milk in a bottle will have the same nutritional benefits as breast-feeding, and modern infant formula preparations are a well-researched source of nutrition for your baby.

EXPRESSED BREAST MILK

There will come a time while breast-feeding when you will need to leave your little one with someone else. Even though you are away from your baby, you can still offer the same benefits of breast milk by expressing and storing breast milk for the feeds. There are a number of reasons why you may need or want to express:

- If your baby is born **prematurely**, he needs the benefits of breast milk as breast milk protects his gut from infection. In the early days many premature babies may not be able to suck from the breast and need to be fed breast milk with a special tube. Your prem baby is likely to stay in hospital after you have been discharged. You can then provide expressed breast milk for his feeds (see page 102).
- You may need to return to **work** soon after the birth of your baby. Working and breast-feeding is possible if you express and store your breast milk. By expressing, you offer not only the benefits of breast milk but will also maintain a constant supply of breast milk so that you can feed your baby when you are around.
- You may just need a **well-deserved break** and by expressing and storing your milk you will be able to leave your baby with dad or a babysitter.

How to express

Expressing breast milk entails extracting milk from your breasts under sterile conditions to feed in a tube or bottle at a later stage. There is no need to be concerned if you can express only small quantities at a time. Your baby is far more efficient at draining your breast than you yourself, or any mechanical aids you may be using to express. Your baby is probably receiving a much larger amount of milk through breast-feeding than you will be able to express in one sitting. You may need to express two or three times to get sufficient milk for one bottle.

HAND-HELD AND ELECTRIC BREAST PUMPS

Breast pumps come in a variety of shapes, sizes and price ranges. You can purchase a pump from a baby store, your clinic sister and some pharmacies, borrow one from a friend who is not using hers at the time, or rent from a maternity unit or clinic. In the beginning when you are trying to establish which pump works well for you, renting or borrowing is a good option until you are set on a certain type.

- Be sure to wash and sterilise the pump and wash your hands thoroughly before expressing. If you are at home, take a hot shower.
- If you are at home, have your baby close by. If you are at work, take along a photo of your baby or listen to a recording of his cries and gurgles.
- Make yourself comfortable in a place where you will not be disturbed and play some relaxing music. It is difficult to express milk if you are feeling tense or uncomfortable – the more relaxed you are the better. Find a comfortable chair and position to sit in. Leaning forward while expressing may help your milk flow.
- Some people manage to express from one breast while feeding baby on the other breast. This is more likely to work once you are comfortable with the breast-feeding position. The advantage is that your letdown reflex is brought on by feeding your baby on the other side.
- Place a warm cloth on your breast. Encourage the letdown reflex by gently massaging your breast with small circles from the top of the breast to nipple area and then place your hands underneath your breast and massage using small circles from the base of the breast to nipple area.
- When placing the pump over the breast ensure the nipple is centred on the suction cup. Start expressing on low suction and then increase speed as you express. Some women have more sensitive nipples than others so the settings will vary according to your needs.

Making it work

STORING BREAST MILK

Breast milk can be kept in sterilised, sealed plastic bottles or containers. Some pumps come with plastic bags that can be sealed with sealing clips. If you are using stored breast milk, label the containers so that first in can be first out.

The following research-based guidelines come from the Australian Association of Breast-feeding Mothers, and are for a mother storing milk at home for a healthy baby. You can store milk:

- At room temperature (25 °C) for up to four hours.
- In a cooler box with ice packs for up to 24 hours.
- In a refrigerator at 4 °C for up to five days.
- In a fridge freezer for up to three months.
- In a chest freezer at a temperature of -20 °C for up to six to twelve months.
- Moved into the refrigerator from the freezer for up to 24 hours in the refrigerator.

FREEZING BREAST MILK

If you are going to freeze breast milk do so within 24 hours of expressing. Although the guidelines say that it can be kept in a chest freezer for six to twelve months, bear in mind that breast milk continually adapts to the growing needs of your baby and milk kept for several months may no longer be suitable to meet your baby's nutritional needs.

Thaw breast milk by removing it from the freezer and put in the refrigerator overnight. To speed up the process, swirl the container of breast milk in warm water. Do not use hot water to thaw breast milk. Thawed breast milk must **never** be refrozen. Any milk left over should be discarded as it may become contaminated. If stored breast milk from the fridge has been heated and only part used, discard the rest.

BOTTLE BASICS

To bottle feed successfully you need the right equipment.

Bottles

There is a huge variety of bottles available and most come complete with a teat and lid. A smaller bottle size (125 ml) may be suitable for younger babies; however larger bottles (250 ml) tend to be a better investment as they can be used right through until your baby is weaned. A range of specialized bottles is also available. These include anti-colic bottles, which assist in reducing the amount of air a baby takes in whilst feeding.

If you are planning to use expressed breast milk in combination with breast-feeding you need two to three bottles. If you are bottle feeding exclusively you need six to eight bottles.

Teats

Teats are either latex or silicone. Latex teats are flesh-coloured and resemble the nipple in texture and are often more readily accepted by breast-fed babies. Be aware that a small number of babies may be allergic to latex. Silicone teats are see-through and tend to last longer as they are stronger.

Breast-fed babies can control the speed at which milk comes out of the nipple – the flow rate – to some extent. A bottle teat has a continuous flow, but teats are categorized by flow rate: slow teats are suitable for newborns, medium for babies of three to six months and fast ones for babies of six months and older. Ensure you choose an appropriate teat for your baby's age.

Teats also vary in shape and can be bell-shaped or more naturally shaped to resemble a nipple. No one shape is better than another, and you should be guided by which one your baby prefers.

narrow   orthodontic

wide   Curity

Bottle brush

Prior to any sterilising you will need to thoroughly clean your baby's bottle using a bottle brush. Some bottle brushes are fitted with a mini brush to clean the teats.

Sterilising equipment

Sterilising your baby's feeding equipment is important in the very early days and if you are living in an area where the water is not clean. As your baby gets older, sterilising is not essential and a good wash in hot soapy water is enough to get rid of the germs.

The germs are spread around through handling with your hands, so wash or spray your hands with alcohol-based disinfectant before preparing the milk and just before you feed your baby.

Your method of sterilising is personal and will depend on how much you want to spend. There are three main methods of sterilising your baby's feeding equipment:

- **Boiling** the bottles and teats in a pot of boiling water on the stove for five minutes.
- Placing the equipment in a tub of **sterilising solution**.
- **Steaming** the bottles on the stove, in a microwave steriliser or even in the dishwasher at the end of a washing cycle.

It is important to note that the minute the sterilisation process for your baby's feeding equipment or dummies ends, especially if they sit for a while or are washed under water or touched by your hands, they are not sterile anymore. Pay attention to keeping your hands clean before and after making the bottle feed. Do not become fastidious about sterilising and certainly don't sterilise your baby's equipment past six months of age – it is simply not necessary. Make sure the equipment is clean and rinsed well.

FORMULA MILK BASICS

For mothers who are unable to breast-feed or who decide not to, infant formula is a good alternative. If you feed your baby a commercially prepared formula, be assured that his nutritional needs will be met.

Emotional aspect

The emotional turmoil that is present in many parenting decisions is amplified in feeding. It therefore does not matter when you introduce formula bottles, at two weeks or twelve months old, the first bottle and last breast-feed are very emotional moments in your parenting journey.

When breast-feeding is challenging you may well find yourself feeling **distress**. You may feel that this is yet another area of parenting where you are letting your baby down and giving substandard care. The reality is that as new moms, we will

---

Formula simulates breast milk as closely as possible and contains the following:

- Omega 3 and Omega 6, essential fats present in breast milk, are now present in most brands and types of baby formula.
- Although there are no Probiotics in breast milk, modern formulas have added Prebiotics and Probiotics, which encourage good stools and growth of healthy bacteria in the colon.
- Antioxidants – these keep the cells healthy.

find any small issue to feel guilty about. Perinatal distress (PND), which encompasses feelings of guilt, sadness, depression and anxiety, can arise at any time in the first few years. Deciding to stop breast-feeding is a common contributor. It is important to know that your decision is the right one for you and your baby. Choose a caregiver or adviser who supports your decision and does not exacerbate your feelings of guilt.

Choosing a formula

While breast-feeding is the best nutrition for babies, commercially prepared infant formulas are a nutritious alternative to breast milk. Manufactured under sterile conditions, commercial formulas attempt to duplicate mother's milk using a complex combination of proteins, sugars, fats, and vitamins that would be virtually impossible to create at home. So, if you don't breast-feed your baby, it's important that you use only a commercially prepared formula.

SENSE-ABLE FEEDING
Only use specially prepared infant formula. Do not be tempted to use:
- Normal powdered milk
- Cow's milk
- Evaporated milk
- Coffee or tea creamer
- Tea

Type of milk	Description	Suitable for
Cow's milk-based formula	Cow's milk base	First choice of formula if you have moved your baby from breast milk
Formula for fussy babies	Less lactose than regular milk-based formula	Babies with some gas or who are very fussy on milk-based formula
Formula for constipated babies	More lactose than regular milk-based formula	Babies with some constipation on milk-based formula
Lactose-free formula	Milk containing no lactose	These should only be used under the guidance of a dietician or paediatrician after a confirmed diagnosis of lactose intolerance (see page 69)
Formula for babies with excessive acid reflux	Thickened formula – note do not use thickening agents	Babies with confirmed reflux that interferes with growth
Soy formula	Soya-based milk	Babies with lactose intolerance, and milk protein allergies, but note that studies show that the use of soy milk or goat's milk formula does not prevent the development of allergies in children
Formula for failing to thrive and low weight gain	Has more protein and calories in the form of healthy fats	Babies who fail to thrive or with very poor weight gain
Formula for premature babies	Has more calories and specific nutrients	Premature and low-birth weight babies
Follow-on formula	Fortified cow's and soya milk	For older infants and toddlers between the ages of 12 and 36 months
Semi-elemental formula	Cow's milk-based formula processed to break down most of the proteins which cause symptoms in infants allergic to cow's milk; also contains a small amount of amino acids	Useful for babies with milk protein and soy allergies

Type of milk	Description	Suitable for
Hypoallergenic formula	Formula with a small amount of protein predigested	Originally designed to reduce the incidence of allergies in high-risk children, very little proven benefit; babies are better off on normal cow's milk based formula or if allergic on a specialised semi-elemental formula or amino acid based formula
Amino acid based formula	Protein is all in the form of amino acids	For babies with milk protein and soy allergies who don't tolerate an elemental formula

SENSE-ABLE FEEDING
Standard cow's milk based formulas are suitable for the majority of babies and are the most commonly used. Before making any formula changes consult your healthcare practitioner.

Formula hopping

If your baby is very irritable, has excessive gas, diarrhoea (which may be bloody), spitting up, vomiting, and shows poor weight gain, he may be intolerant to the formula he is on.

Choosing another type of baby formula, in consultation with a dietician, nursing sister or paediatrician, may help alleviate the symptoms. Simply changing brands, unless you also change formula types, does not usually make a difference. You should not self-diagnose your baby's problems and simply switch formula. You are more likely to create further problems by uninformed formula switching. If you have a problem you think is related to your baby's formula, speak to your doctor or clinic sister.

Preparing formula milk

Unlike breast milk which is always on tap, formula feeds need to be planned in advance so that you are not caught with no milk, sterile water or worse, out and about, with nothing to feed your baby.

- Preboil water and decant the right amount into bottles; keep this water so that you always have cooled boiled water available.
- When travelling, take with you at least two formula feeds in powder form with two bottles with the right amount of boiled water.

SENSE-ABLE FEEDING
Always follow the directions for mixing the formula provided on the tin. By adding more scoops or more water than recommended you place your baby's nutrition and his kidneys at risk.

When making up a bottle using formula, follow these guidelines:

- Boil fresh water and let it cool to room temperature or slightly warmer and pour the required amount into the bottle
- Add the exact number of scoops specified on the packaging. Always use the scoop provided by the manufacturer. Level each scoop of powder using a knife and add it to the bottle.
- Place the teat as well as the lid on the bottle and secure.
- Shake the bottle until all the powder has dissolved.
- Test the temperature of the bottle and cool down under cold water if necessary before feeding your baby.

Storing prepared milk

A bottle of prepared formula can be stored in the fridge for a maximum of 24 hours and must be used within that period of time. Once reheated, you must discard whatever is left over after the feed. You can only heat milk once after preparation.

The preferable way to heat milk is to stand the bottle in a mug of warm water. If you use a microwave:

- Ensure the formula is well mixed before placing in the microwave
- Only heat for a few seconds to avoid overheating and destroying the nutrients
- Always give the milk a shake after heating in the microwave to ensure even heating.

Regardless of heating method, ensure the milk is not too warm for your baby by testing it on your inner arm or wrist.

SENSORY ASPECTS OF BOTTLE FEEDING

Sucking on a teat – be it silicone or latex – is a novel sensory experience for your baby. Many babies become resistant to new textures or methods of feeding as they get older. This is particularly true for sensitive babies who do not readily tolerate new textures in their mouths. In the event that you have an emergency when your baby needs to be bottle fed, you will want to have the option of bottle feeding open to you. Therefore it is worth introducing a bottle to your baby at six weeks, and then offer a bottle of expressed breast milk every two or three weeks, even if you plan to breast-feed exclusively.

Like breast-feeding, bottle feeding is not simply a method of delivering nutrition to your baby. Bottle feeding is a sensory and emotional experience too.

Touch

Always hold your baby for a bottle feed. Touch your baby, stroke his hair and caress his skin. At feed time, unwrap him and allow his hands to be free to **touch** your chest, neck or face. Unbutton your top and encourage your little one to touch and feel your skin whilst bottle feeding.

Hearing

Talk to your baby and hold him close so he can hear your heartbeat. Speak to him in an even, soothing **voice.**

Sight

Make eye contact and have your baby focus on your face. Learn to read his **signals** while he is feeding. For example, if he makes eye contact, reciprocate, but follow suit if he looks away. This will allow him 'sensory space' to focus on the task at hand.

Position sense

Hold your baby in a horizontal feeding position, similar to that of breast-feeding. Avoid feeding your baby in a baby chair with the bottle propped in his mouth.

Smell

The smell of your 'mother space' will be soothing during feeds. Do not wear perfume for the early months of your baby's life. During that time, your baby is in very close proximity to you at a time when **smell** is important – while he is feeding. Your own body smell is the most neutral and best for your baby.

Some babies have difficulty coordinating **sucking, swallowing and breathing** in the presence of other stimulation. If your baby is a *sensitive baby*, limit any extra-sensory input while he's feeding. If you choose to talk to him, do so quietly and calmly. Keep your touch a still, deep hug. If your baby is a difficult feeder, try swaddling him for the feeds.

WEANING YOUR BABY

The process of switching your baby to bottle feeding may take place over a few days or be stretched out to a few months. It need not be a tricky business if you are sensible about your approach to it. There are three ways to wean your baby:

- **Slow process** over months in which you breast-feed for nine months or more and slowly introduce your baby to a sippy or straw cup, which will eventually take the place of your breast-feeds.
- **Intermediate process** – weaning your baby from breast to bottle over a period of a few weeks to months, by replacing one breast-feed at a time. This may be at any stage – from a few weeks old to closer to a year. If you are returning to work, it is possible to wean your baby within a week or so, depending on how much you are feeding.
- **Cold turkey** – necessary if you need to stop overnight for medical reasons

Slow process

If your baby is nine months old he should be down to three feeds a day. The afternoon milk feed can be replaced by a cup feed as this feed will be dropped by a year. Thereafter all liquids can be given in a sippy or straw cup. Over time your last feed of the day, which is usually the evening feed at 18 months, is also a cup of milk before bed.

Intermediate process

On the first day, substitute a bottle for one breast-feed. It is wise to choose a feed that is either at a convenient time for you, when you are away from your baby, or one that is less special to you. The mid-morning or mid-afternoon feed is a good idea. If possible, have someone other than yourself give the bottle. You may even need to be in another room or out of the house altogether. Choose a bottle and teat your feel comfortable with and prepare and heat the formula as discussed on page 38. Use a bottle at this feed for at least two days, but you can continue with only one formula feed for as long as you wish.

Next, increase the number of bottles to two feeds for two days or as long as you wish to continue. By now both the mid-afternoon and mid-morning feeds (if your baby still has both feeds) will be bottles.

Thereafter, keep replacing one breast-feed every third day or as long as you wish to continue until your baby is exclusively bottle-fed.

Use the same method to wean your baby from a bottle to a sippy or straw cup once he is old enough.

Cold turkey

The critical elements to stopping breast-feeding your baby overnight is to manage your baby's needs and your comfort:

- *Your baby* – You will need a helpful partner to assist with the feeds to meet your baby's need for touch, and extra love and contact.
- *Your comfort* – You will undoubtedly need medication to dry up your milk supply. Your doctor will prescribe such medication to reduce the possibility of breast engorgement and infection (mastitis).

Pain-free weaning

Each feed you drop will continue to be produced by your breasts for a few days. This means your breasts may well end up feeling full and possibly painful. To manage the discomfort, try the following:

- Cabbage leaves: If you are weaning your baby, place several fresh cabbage leaves in your bra (replacing every three hours) to manage the pain.
- Warm showers: When engorgement becomes painful, try taking a warm shower. With your back to the spray, allow the water to flow over your shoulders and down your chest. To relieve the pressure you can express a small amount of milk with your hands. This method will not stimulate more milk production, but will help to manage the discomfort during weaning.
- Fluid restriction: Begin to decrease the amount of liquids you drink by half. This will assist in reducing the amount of milk you produce.
- Do not pump: Do not replace a bottle feeding with pumping or expressing if you wish to reduce milk production.

CHAPTER 4

Solids

*Lisa had this mothering story all sorted. She had focused on a good diet in preg-
nancy and had a sense of accomplishment as she breast-fed Bella – a settled little
girl who fed well and slept like a dream. But soon after Bella hit four months of
age, things changed dramatically. She began to demand a feed every two hours
and was waking at night again. At first Lisa thought Bella was experiencing a
growth spurt and fed her more frequently. After a month she found herself in
a never-ending cycle of breast-feeding every two hours for very long periods of
time, and Bella was waking repeatedly at night. Lisa had heard she should introduce solids when Bella needed them, but had no idea when that was and, in fact,
was getting very conflicting advice on how to introduce solids.*

Just when you feel you have mastered breast or bottle feeding, the next parenting challenge will present itself: when to introduce solids and what constitutes a
healthy diet for your baby. Trends change almost every decade when it comes
to solids. In the 1970s, parents were encouraged to introduce solids such as
strained oats and even avocado as early as six weeks of age. In the 1990s the
advice was not to introduce solids until after six months of age. Some mothers
even thought that the later the better and battled on with milk alone for much
of the first year of their baby's life.

THE RIGHT TIME FOR SOLIDS

Much of the debate on *when* to introduce solids has centred on when a baby
is ready to digest food other than milk and what age is best to limit the risk of
allergies developing. The latest research presented in 2008 and 2009 shows that
delaying the introduction of solids beyond six months may play a role in *increasing* the risk of fussy eating, allergies and nutritional deficiencies. This has changed
the recommendations on solids by organizations such as the American Pediatric
Association and the European Food Safety Authority. There are specific criteria
to be considered when deciding when to introduce solids:

Is my baby developmentally ready?

Between four and six months of age, many developmental changes indicate that
your baby is growing into a social little person and is becoming ready for solid food:

REFLEXES

At birth protective reflexes exist that become integrated as your baby grows. Three
of the reflexes that impact on eating solid foods are the gag, sucking and tongue
thrust reflexes. At birth the gag reflex is very strong, which is a good thing as it pro-

tects your newborn from choking – if something more solid than milk touches your baby's soft palate, she will gag and in that way protect her airway and throat from anything going down. Likewise, her tongue thrust reflex prevents anything that she could choke on from getting into her mouth, as her tongue pushes any foreign textures out of her mouth. Her sucking and rooting reflexes are vital for the establishment of breast-feeding. These reflexes respond to touch on the tongue and cheek respectively and ensure your baby will turn towards a soft nipple and begin to suck when the nipple is in her mouth. Only once all these reflexes are integrated should you consider solid foods. The sucking and tongue thrust reflexes are integrated at around four months of age, when sucking becomes intentional. The gag reflex persists into adulthood but between four and six months of age, diminishes sufficiently that most babies can swallow mushy solid food without gagging.

REACHING
Your baby will begin to reach for things – your food, necklace and a toy are all interesting and she can coordinate reaching out to grasp something and getting it to her mouth. Whilst sitting on your lap at a meal, she will reach for your spoon.

HEAD CONTROL
In order to feed on solid food, your baby must be able to hold her head up with ease. By four to five months of age she should be able to sit on your lap supported around the waist, and hold her head up while watching your face.

SOCIAL
Your four to six month-old is a little social butterfly and enjoys social interaction during feeding time. No longer is your baby focused just on satisfying her appetite, she will lose interest in the breast quickly during a feed and the social aspect of eating emerges.

INTEREST
Your baby will begin to show great interest in the things you are doing. When sitting on your lap at mealtimes, she will watch you eat and take food to your mouth. During this time she will probably begin to reach out for your spoon or cup and express an interest in doing what mommy is doing.

When your baby begins to show these developmental milestones, you know that she is ready for solid foods. This does not mean you will automatically introduce solids as you will consider many other factors. However, you should **not** introduce solids until your baby is developmentally ready.

Nutritional readiness

Between four and six months of age, many of the nutrient stores that your baby was born with will become depleted. The closer she gets to six months, the milk she is drinking will no longer meet all her nutritional demands as she grows. While milk remains the primary source of food in the first few months of solid foods, only solid foods can fill the gaps of specific nutrients that are now needed in greater quantities.

Late introduction of solids, after six months of age, may result in iron, energy or protein deficiency and your baby's growth and weight gain may also be affected. On the other hand, early introduction of solids – before four months – may lead to accelerated weight gain which could have long-term negative consequences like an increased risk of obesity and type 2 diabetes later in life. The optimal age to introduce solids in terms of nutritional readiness is between four and six months of age. You will know your baby is nutritionally ready when:

- Her normal milk feeds no longer satisfy her – she will be demanding bottle feeds more frequently than three- to four-hourly and breast-feeds more than 2½ to three-hourly for more than one to two weeks.
- Her growth starts to slow down over a period of a month.
- She is more active and mobile, using more energy.
- Her sleeping patterns at night are disrupted and she may start to wake more frequently after a period of sleeping well.

Allergies

You can safely introduce solids to your baby after 17 weeks for a full-term baby (or 17 weeks corrected age for a prem baby) without placing her at any greater risk of developing food allergies or eczema than if left for later. You can also introduce high-risk allergy foods from six months of age without placing your baby at any allergy risk. If your baby is predisposed to allergies, introduce the allergen foods (egg, dairy, fish, nuts, wheat and gluten) one at a time to assess any reaction. Delaying the introduction will not reduce the chance of a reaction if your baby is going to react to a certain food. By delaying introduction beyond seven to nine months you are actually placing your baby at a greater risk of having a reaction to these foods when eventually introduced.

SOLIDS: THE RIGHT TOOLS

As you prepare to introduce solid food to your baby, ensure that you have basic, sensible feeding equipment.

Spoons

Consider your baby's feeding experience up to this point: she has been obtaining her food by sucking from a soft nipple, nuzzled in your chest and enfolded in your arms – your nipple is soft and familiar and bottle teats are similarly shaped, soft and pliable. Suddenly your little one is expected to sit up, separate from her mom, and open her mouth to receive unfamiliar solid food offered on a foreign, hard piece of equipment – the feeding spoon. For this reason choose the spoon wisely. Cartoon characters may look cute but mean nothing to her until the toddler years. A hard metal spoon is cold and unwelcome in her little mouth. A spoon that is too deep and too wide makes this new experience all the more challenging.

The ideal starter spoon is simple in shape, with a soft, flat scoop that allows your baby to suck the food off the spoon initially. From there she can graduate to a more normal looking spoon with a more solid texture. Avoid spoons that are too deep, too hard, and covered in plastic as opposed to solid plastic.

Chairs

As soon as your baby can sit upright, you can use a high-chair. A simple high-chair that is safe and has a tray table is more than adequate. It may be helpful to find a chair that you can easily fold up and transport to granny's house for dinner. Most babies are ready to sit in a high-chair by five to six months. Some of the things you need to consider when shopping for a high-chair are cost, ease of cleaning, stability when standing, removable front tray, washable and padded linings, appropriate 'chair belt' harness.

- Never leave your baby unattended when she is in her high-chair.
- Keep your baby's high-chair away from plug points, stoves or other potentially harmful appliances.
- Check that she is properly secured in the chair
- Discourage playing around high-chair beyond mealtimes. It is not a jungle gym.
- Be mindful of little fingers when you remove the tray or unfasten the clasps.

Bibs

Bibs are essential to protect clothing during mealtimes and since we want mealtimes to be a fun and messy experience, bibs will come in handy. Fabric bibs, with a soft waterproof backing that cover your baby's upper body and have a press stud to attach, are most convenient. These are generally easy to put on and remove and are easy to wash.

Drinking cups

Use bottles for milk, not for water and juice. There is a wide range of cup choices for weaning your baby from breast or bottle onto a normal plastic beaker:

- **Sippy cups** are useful for your baby's transition from a bottle to a normal drinking cup and to use for tea or water from about six months onwards. A sippy cup has a plastic spout of any shape or description from which your baby will suck the liquid. It still requires sucking and therefore can contribute to tooth decay if sweetened liquids are consumed; especially if this is used before sleep times once teeth have emerged. Choose a sippy cup with a soft spout that can be easily cleaned.
- A **straw cup** is not only good for oral-motor development but also prevents juice pooling in the mouth, which encourages tooth decay.

Most babies can learn to suck from a straw by nine months of age. To start, offer infant or toddler juice (which has lower sugar content) in a carton with a straw. This will be easy to squeeze lightly as your baby plays with the straw with her mouth. She will quickly realize that a little suck is followed by the reward of juice and within no time will learn to suck a straw cup.

- By the time your baby is a year old, you should encourage her to drink from a **normal cup** or a **straw cup** to prevent tooth decay. Use the sippy cup for water when you are in the car to avoid spills.

A NUTRITIOUS DIET

One of your biggest responsibilities as a parent is to provide your baby with a healthy, balanced diet that will help her grow into a healthy child and eventually a healthy adult with good eating habits. Your child's diet and the rate at which she grows between the ages of two and 12 can have a major effect on her predisposition to obesity and chronic diseases later in life. When you start weaning your baby onto solid food, it is very important that you know what you are aiming for with regards to her health and nutrition.

A nutritious diet in childhood will include the following:
- A wide variety of foods
- Three meals a day and two to three nutritious snacks
- A range of foods containing cereals and starch, such as rice, pasta, potatoes and wholegrain bread
- Plenty of fruit and vegetables
- A range of dairy foods
- Meat, chicken, fish, beans, soya or peanut butter daily
- Regular drinks of clean water
- A sufficient intake of foods high in essential fatty acids
- Only small amounts of fast foods, sweets or sugary drinks

Mealtime suggestions that will lead to healthy eating patterns
- Don't force-feed your child
- Eat meals together as a family
- Avoid rewards, threats and coercion to get your child to eat
- Allow your child (baby and toddler) to listen to her body and control the amount of food she eats

Variety of foods

Expose your baby to a range of different food textures, tastes and flavours from an early age. Exposure doesn't necessarily mean swallowing the food — it is a multisensory experience and leads to acceptance of food.
- Your baby will play with and *touch* her food.
- Encourage her to *smell* the food on the spoon or in the bowl and comment on the smells in the kitchen.
- Don't be scared to give her *tastes* of the food from your plate, exposing her to varied and stronger flavours from six months onwards.
- *Look* at pictures of different foods: make a little food book from magazine pictures of food and 'read' it with your baby.
- Your breast-fed baby is exposed to all the food flavours that you enjoy and it is important to reinforce these flavours when you introduce solids into her diet.

Before six months of age: When introducing solids, include variety by offering new foods gradually.

Six months to the toddler years: This is the stage when you can really offer a wide variety of flavours and textures, and homemade foods will give you the best opportunity to do so. Acceptance of a wide variety of flavours and textures is the key to a non-fussy eater later.

Toddlers: They go through stages when they eat a very limited range of flavours and textures. This fussy eating stage is normal. Keep offering variety but don't force your toddler to eat food she is resistant to.

Regular meals and snacks

While it is ideal to eat according to hunger, this is not always practical in a world where schedules and routines are part of life. If meals and snacks are given at the same time every day, you will find that your baby's body easily adjusts to an eating routine. By offering three regular meals and two to three nutritious snacks you allow your baby many feeding opportunities. If she eats very little breakfast one day, you can relax knowing she will be offered a mid-morning snack and another opportunity to eat healthy food.

SENSE-ABLE FEEDING
If you move into a sense-able feeding routine when you start your baby on solids, it will be a comfortable way of life by the time you get to those fussy toddler years.

Before six months of age: By the time you introduce solids, your baby will be ready for a feeding routine. Chapters 10-12 include specific meal plans for your baby.

Six months to the toddler years: Over time you will reduce your baby's milk feeds until she has three meals and two snacks a day with milk feeds taking a back seat and eventually being dropped almost entirely.

Toddlers: Toddlers do not grow as fast as babies, and your toddler may start to eat a little more erratically. It is perfectly normal for a child between one and five years to eat all her daily food requirements at one meal and then very little at the next meals. She may also eat small bits throughout the day. By offering her five planned opportunities to eat (three meals and two snacks), she will be more likely to meet her requirements.

SENSE-ABLE FEEDING
Gluten, a protein in rye, wheat, oats and barley, must be introduced after four but before seven months to reduce the risk of celiac disease later in life. Celiac disease causes damage to the intestines when gluten is eaten. It can lead to iron deficiency and iron deficiency anaemia because of bleeding from the small intestine.

Range of grains and starchy foods

Breads, rice cereals and pasta are grains. Grains such as rice, wheat, oats and barley, millet, corn and rye can be whole or ground. The main benefit of eating grains is the carbohydrate content which provides the body with energy that can be stored. Grains are also a good source of iron and vitamin B. Starchy vegetables like potatoes are also good sources of carbohydrates.

Whole grains contain large amounts of fibre. Fibre has many benefits including removing toxic waste through the colon. This promotes the growth of healthy bacteria (probiotics) and strengthens your baby's immunity.

Before six months of age: Single grain cereals, such as rice or maize cereal, will probably be one of your baby's first solid foods. These grains have added iron and fill your baby up nicely. Recent research has shown that the introduction of gluten foods prior to seven months of age helps reduce the risk of celiac disease.

Six months to the toddler years: Most babies love the white foods like oats, barley, pasta, mashed potatoes and rice – these are great basic foods that should be part of each meal.

Toddlers: Some toddlers end up eating almost only the 'whites' – bread, pasta and cereal. Guard against encouraging your toddler to fill up on starches only as she needs a variety of foods.

Plenty of fresh fruit and vegetables

Fruit and vegetables contain many vitamins, minerals, fibre and carbohydrates which give your baby energy. Fruit and vegetables are vital for your baby's immunity and health.

Before six months of age: Start with steamed vegetables puréed until smooth. Later you can introduce smooth steamed fruit purée as a sweet flavour in yogurt or as a pudding after a veggie meal.

Six months to the toddler years: A wide range of fruit and vegetables is essential now. Offer at least two types of steamed or raw vegetable per meal. Fruit after meals and as snacks provides the variety needed for your baby's health.

Toddlers: Toddlers may develop very strong preferences for certain foods, especially with fruit and vegetables. If you find your toddler will only eat fruit and disdains any form of vegetable, don't worry. She will get her vitamin requirements from fruit. Keep offering the vegetables at meals and in time she will get a taste for them.

Range of dairy

Dairy foods include milk, cheese and yogurt and are a rich source of calcium – a very important mineral that helps build healthy teeth and bones. These foods are also a good source of carbohydrates, fat and protein, as well as some vitamins. Up to the age of two, your little one should have full-cream milk and dairy products. Thereafter offer low-fat options.

Before six months of age: Dairy, other than a cow's milk formula, may be introduced in limited forms prior to six months. Add yogurt or cottage cheese to your baby's diet once she has been on solids for a month or so.

Six months to the toddler years: All dairy can be introduced after six months of age and by the time your baby is one year old, you can stop using infant formulas and use regular full-cream cow's milk in her tea or bottles.

Toddlers: They generally love dairy – yogurt, cheese and milky tea are firm favourites with most toddlers and provide them with protein, calcium and some essential fatty acids.

Meat, chicken, fish, eggs, soya and beans

These foods have a high nutritional value and are an excellent source of iron and protein. Protein is broken down into essential amino acids, which help your baby's body to build healthy muscles and other body tissues. Protein is also important for your baby to feel satisfied after a meal. The energy from a meal that contains protein will be released slowly, helping your baby feel full for longer. Use lean meat and chicken with all visible fat removed. Grill, bake or roast meat, chicken and fish.

Before six months of age: It is generally accepted that meats and proteins other than milk should not be introduced prior to six months of age.

Six months to the toddler years: By six months of age, your baby needs the essential amino acids and iron found in meat and other proteins and you should introduce them now. Introduce one protein food at a time. Allow two to three days to watch for any negative effect of this particular food before introducing a new protein food.

Toddlers: Toddlers often like one or two specific proteins and normally ones that are not too difficult to chew. Offer dairy and soya products to help meet your toddler's protein needs.

VEGETARIAN DIET

One of the most important reasons to introduce meat is for the protein it provides. Along with meat, some excellent sources of protein are eggs, nuts and dairy products. Protein is also found in legumes such as beans, peas and lentils, some vegetables, grains and fruits, though many of these sources of protein are considered incomplete proteins because they do not contain enough or all the amino acids.

Introducing meat into your baby's diet before 12 months of age, if at all, is an entirely personal decision. Meat is not essential in your baby's diet, but **protein** is. Make sure you offer foods that contain both the complete and the incomplete proteins, for example peanut butter and bread, black beans and rice, cottage cheese and avocado, milk and a grain cereal, egg and bread. In this way she will receive all the necessary proteins without ever having to eat meat.

A vegetarian diet may lack sufficient iron and vitamin B12 and you have to ensure that your baby has an adequate supplement of these and other vitamins and minerals. If you choose a vegetarian diet for your baby, it is advisable to consult with a registered dietician.

Regular intake of water

Without water, your body would stop working properly. Your baby's body has lots of important jobs and it needs water to do many of them. Her blood, which contains a lot of water, carries oxygen to all the cells in her body. Without oxygen, those tiny cells would die and her body would stop working. Water is important in the digestion of food and to get rid of waste, too.

Lots of foods contain water, so your baby will get some of her water intake through solid food. Fruit has a high water content, which you could probably tell if you've ever bitten into a peach or plum and felt the juices dripping down your chin! Vegetables, too, contain a lot of water. Naturally, any fluid your baby drinks contains water, but clean tap or boiled water and milk are the best choices.

Before six months of age: While you are exclusively breast-feeding, your baby does not need any liquids other than breast milk. Even in hot weather, your milk will adjust to provide more thirst quenching foremilk to satisfy your baby's thirst. If your baby is on formula milk and once you begin the weaning process, you have to offer your baby thirst-quenching water and later introduce other drinks too. For babies under six months of age, you can give boiled tap water. Bottled water isn't a healthier choice than tap water and usually isn't sterile. In very hot weather, offer your baby some cooled boiled water in a bottle. Water must never be offered as a substitute for milk in your baby's first year of life.

Six months to the toddler years: By giving your baby juices and other drinks you may reduce her appetite for milk. Fruit juice also contains sugars which can cause tooth decay. As your baby approaches her first birthday, you can introduce small quantities of diluted fruit juice (1 part fruit juice to 10 parts water). Focus on water in the first two years and offer fruit juice as an occasional treat. Once your baby is on a diet of solids you can introduce caffeine-free tea. Rooibos tea with cow's milk (70 ml tea to 30 ml milk) after the age of 12 months will be a welcome addition to her liquid range. You can offer a younger baby cooled Rooibos tea without milk after solids in hot weather, as long as it does not detract from milk intake.

Toddlers: Having water 'on tap' for your toddler creates a healthy habit of choosing water for thirst. A daily cup of milk, 1-2 cups of Rooibos tea, ½ cup of fruit juice and as much water as she wants will be adequate.

Essential fatty acids

Fat is a concentrated source of energy and the essential fats play an important role in brain development and the immune system. The two main essential fats are Omega 3 and Omega 6. While your baby is on breast milk she receives all her essential fatty acids and most formulas are also fortified with essential fats. Once your baby is on solids, Omega 6 is ingested in sufficient quantities in a healthy diet, but Omega 3 fats are more of a challenge. Eventually in the weaning process you will introduce your baby to nuts and seeds, fatty fish and certain oils to ensure that she gets all the essential fatty acids.

Before six months of age: Breast milk and most infant formulas contain sufficient essential fats to meet your baby's needs and as she is on an almost exclusive milk diet at this stage, added fats are not necessary.

Six months to the toddler years: During this stage you can introduce a variety of healthy fats including some fatty fish and healthy oils (see Chapter 13 for examples).

Toddlers: For fussy toddlers, fatty foods such as avocado, nuts, and olive or canola oil offer a good source of energy for less quantity. After two years it is not important to give full-cream dairy products; low fat will be fine.

Limit fast foods and sugary snacks

These include cakes, biscuits, chocolates, sweets, ice cream, potato chips and many others – foods that your baby doesn't need. You often find these foods in the checkout line at the supermarket just in reach of your young toddler's grasp. Generally they contain high levels of refined sugars, salt and fats. A child who eats a lot of these foods will not receive all the nutrition she needs and is not learning about good nutrition. We call these foods empty energy foods as they provide energy without the vitamins, minerals, fibre and so on. Your baby does not need these foods at all in the first year of weaning and your toddler should only be exposed to them in moderation as an occasional treat. It is important to expose your toddler to these foods in a very relaxed, casual manner on occasion as it teaches her to moderate her intake and not gorge herself on 'forbidden foods' at the numerous birthday parties she will be invited to.

Take-away or convenience foods also fall into this category. Use them with caution as it is often difficult to assess their nutritional value. This time of weaning your baby is a good opportunity to assess your eating habits as you now are in a teaching position and the old adage 'monkey see, monkey do' holds very true when it comes to eating habits. You may want to re-assess the frequency of your visits to the take-away shop and find healthier alternatives for those nights when you just can't manage a home-cooked meal. Setting boundaries is a good start. For example, Saturday night is take-away night, or we have pudding on a Wednesday night. This will help you when your little one starts to push the boundaries.

SENSE-ABLE FEEDING
Do not place a total embargo on sweets and snacks as this may make them all the more desirable for your toddler.

Food can be considered organic if no artificial chemicals were used during the production, growth or harvest of the product. The term is also applied to animal products, including meat and dairy items. A benefit of organic foods, notably organic produce, is their high nutritional content. In some cases, organic fruits and vegetables may contain vitamins, minerals, and nutrients that may be lost when the crops are farmed conventionally.

Eating organic foods is also an easy way to avoid genetically modified food (GMF). During the production of GMF allergens from specific plants could be transferred into others, meaning that you may not know if the corn or potatoes you are buying contain a gene from a peanut – something that many people are allergic to.

It is important to note that the production of GMF requires less pesticide and herbicide than regular non-GMF produce. In view of these and other benefits, the GMF debate continues.

FOOD FADS

For past generations, eating was a matter of survival and availability. In recent times, with the wide reach of media and in particular the Internet, food has taken on a new dimension. People no longer consume food to fulfil a basic physiological need – instead, eating has become a symbol of our lifestyle. Trends in nutrition are more prevalent than ever before. Everyone is an expert in nutrition, dishing out advice, and could make weaning your baby and feeding your family a confusing and challenging task. Keep it simple when it comes to feeding your baby. Go back to basics, avoid hopping from one trend to another. Draw on one or two credible sources of nutritional information and filter out anything else. Avoid the following feeding trends, especially when it comes to your baby:
- Not eating fruit with your meals
- Not combining protein and carbohydrates
- Veganism (no animal products including dairy and eggs)
- Feeding your baby only green vegetables
- Avoiding fats in your baby's diet

SUPPLEMENTS

Nutritional supplements are a massive industry and when needed these are very beneficial for ill babies and those failing to thrive. The question is when should we give supplements to normal healthy babies and toddlers?

If your baby is growing and developing normally you do not need to give her an additional **vitamin supplement**. Very young babies should **never** be given a vitamin supplement without medical advice. Your baby will get all the vitamins and nutrients she needs from her milk as well as a range of healthy foods. If you are concerned that your older baby and especially your toddler is not eating particular foods, seek guidance from a health professional with regards to specific supplements.

You may find yourself wanting to supplement to boost immunity when your toddler starts a playgroup or your baby has to go to crèche (when you go back to work). In these cases a good general **multivitamin** that meets 50-80% of your little one's vitamin and mineral needs will be a good option. Giving your child a vitamin holiday or a break from the supplement over weekends is advisable to prevent certain vitamins and minerals building up to toxic levels.

If your child is no longer breast-feeding or on a formula with all the essential fatty acids and her diet does not contain fish, nuts, avocado and other foods rich in fats, you should give her an **essential fatty acid supplement**. There are many options, so consult a health professional to ensure you choose the right Omega 3 supplement for your child.

Premature babies will be given a **multivitamin** and **iron supplement** as their stores of these nutrients will be lower than those of a full-term baby.

There is currently a trend to offer babies protein supplements in the form of powder added to food or formula, often in an attempt to get them to sleep through the night. While it is true that a well-balanced diet including adequate protein after six months of age does help babies sleep for longer stretches, it is important that your baby gets this protein from her normal diet.

Protein is broken down by the kidneys and too much protein (from supplements) can put your baby's little kidneys under strain by overworking them. No mom should administer any protein supplement except under the specific guidance of a healthcare professional who is trained to calculate her baby's requirements. In some instances additional energy in the form of fat and glucose powders may be required in combination with protein to ensure an accurate and constant ratio of all these nutrients. If so, the quantities need to be calculated very carefully.

Seek the opinion of a registered dietician to address this concern in the following cases:

- If your baby was born prematurely and is growing poorly she *may* need additional calories over and above her normal food and milk intake.
- If your baby has special needs as a result of genetic defects, cerebral palsy, or failure to thrive.

Feeding problems

John was Anna's third baby and by the time he came along she was considered a real expert on parenting. As a mother of two and a physiotherapist who dealt with children all day in her busy practice, she was not fazed by the birth of her third child. But the road had not been smooth sailing. Within a few weeks, she realized that John had severe reflux. Her paediatrician had been amazing, seeing her through reflux and weight gain issues and later picking up that John had serious allergies, which were the trigger for many of his problems. It had been a long, hard road, yet when Anna looked back she realized that she had all the support she needed, so her self-esteem as a mom had not been destroyed. But she could well imagine how even one of these feeding issues could throw any parent off kilter!

There is undoubtedly no area of parenting that causes as much anxiety and distress as a baby who won't eat and is not thriving. Emotionally, this challenge may haunt you for years to come. The advice in this chapter is for parents who have battled from day one with real feeding issues, as well as those whose woes only arise in the toddler years. It is well researched and is the same advice you would get if visiting this team of experts: a clinical dietician, a paediatrician and an occupational therapist.

If your baby has feeding problems, they will manifest in a specific concern:

- Your baby may be a **fussy eater** and you may be concerned that you cannot meet his nutritional requirements as a result.
- Your baby may have **poor weight gain or be underweight**. If his weight is dropping or you have always battled to increase his weight off a low base you are justifiably concerned.
- Your baby may be **overweight** and experiencing a dramatic weight gain which will also be cause for concern.
- Your baby may have a feeding problem owing to a **physical limitation** he has been born with.
- You may have a **personal** reason why feeding your baby is an area of difficulty.

FUSSY FEEDING

If your baby is a fussy eater, you may find you dread each feed or meal. You may find your breast-feeding baby suddenly starts fussing at the breast or that your seven month-old won't open his mouth for solids, or that your toddler refuses everything but white foods. Fussy feeding at any stage creates anxiety for mom. There are reasons behind each stage of fussy eating that can be addressed to make your road smoother.

Reflux

If your baby is positing large amounts of milk and is very unsettled after and even during feeds, is a poor sleeper and has low weight gain, he may be suffering from acid reflux. Gastro-oesophageal reflux refers to the regurgitation of stomach contents and acid from the stomach up the oesophagus, usually resulting in bringing up milk or 'vomiting'. There are degrees of reflux and it is important to note the different levels and when to be concerned:

- *Posit:* This refers to spitting up milk when burping or breaking wind after a feed. This is not abnormal even if it occurs after every feed. Your baby will bring up a small amount of milk, which spills onto his bib or makes a small mark on his bed clothes. This is common and completely normal if your baby grows well.
- *Physiological reflux:* Some babies posit large amounts after every feed. This type of positing can be forceful and it may look like your baby has posited up his entire feed. As long as your baby is happy and feeding well and has no signs of illness and is growing and developing normally, you need not be concerned, even if he is positing great volumes of milk.
- *Pathological reflux:* Occasionally reflux is so severe that it leads to failure to thrive. In this case your baby does not grow adequately and is weak and feeding poorly or is very unsettled. The stomach acid may damage the lower end of the oesophagus, leading to burning and ulceration of the oesophagus. Severe reflux can also lead to frequent chest and upper respiratory tract infections and these add to the poor health and growth of your baby. This severity of reflux needs to be diagnosed and managed by a doctor.

MANAGING REFLUX

If your baby is **positing** large amounts of milk even if he is well, it is understandable that you may be very concerned and really want the positing to stop. To manage reflux:

- Feed him **smaller amounts** more frequently.
- Keep him **upright** after feeds and raise the head of his cot so that his head is higher than his feet whilst sleeping.
- Reflux in bottle-fed babies can sometimes be managed by using **anti-reflux formulas**.
- Do not use thickener or cereal in milk.

If your baby has physiological reflux, no further medication is required and the severe positing will stop between six months and one year of age when he is more mobile and is upright and walking around.

If your baby has pathological reflux, is very unsettled and is not gaining weight, he does need further examination and treatment. In addition to all the aforementioned measures, your baby may also require **medication** (such as antacids or proton pump inhibitors) to neutralise the stomach acid and prevent irritation of the lower oesophagus.

Surgery is the last option, only if medication does not help. The operation tightens the lower end of the oesophagus where it enters the stomach and this stops the movement of the stomach contents and the acid up the oesophagus. The operation requires admission to hospital and a general anaesthetic.

Food refusal

Food refusal may arise at any time. You may find when introduced to solids your little one pushes the food from is mouth. Learning to eat solids is similar to learning any new skill. It requires patience and you must accept that some meals may be skipped in the early days of solid introduction. Manage your expectations and make sure they are reasonable when it comes to quantity and variety. Many little ones appear to refuse food in the early days; your baby may open his mouth but as soon as the food is in, will push it back out.

MANAGING EARLY FOOD REFUSAL

If you have just started solids and your baby is refusing food, it may be that he is not quite ready.

- Stop offering him the solids for a few days or even a week and then try again. If he is already six months old, he needs to be introduced to solids so delay only until the next day.
- Feeding your baby off your finger may be more appealing for him than a foreign spoon. Allowing him to play, touch and feel the food will help him get used to this new experience.

MANAGING FOOD REFUSAL DURING THE FIRST YEAR

As your baby gets older you may find that food refusal is more specific to what he is being offered and the time of day.

- Babies are unique and some babies will be happy to stick with the same food for months, whereas others may need **more variety** and have more varied taste preferences. Try something that is totally different if your once happy solid feeder is now refusing his meals. This may be an indication that he wants to try new tastes, textures and flavours.
- If your baby is drinking too much milk in a 24-hour period he will understandably not have much of an appetite for solids. This is especially true if your baby is still being offered milk at night after six months of age. Limit your baby's milk consumption according to the guidelines discussed in Chapter 13 (page 143).
- A **tired baby** is more likely to refuse food than a happily awake baby. Feed your baby whilst in the calm-alert state.
- If your baby has been eating solids well and then suddenly refuses them, he may be **ill or teething**. Sick babies, like adults, don't necessarily feel like eating. (See Chapter 7 on illness affecting appetite**.)** As long as your baby is drinking sufficient liquid a few days of no solids will not harm him. Resume solids slowly once you see your baby is well.

MANAGING FOOD REFUSAL IN THE TODDLER YEARS

A toddler is a different being when it comes to eating and food refusals are as common as temper tantrums. Your toddler may refuse to eat something simply **because he can**. He may well be refusing food or saying "no" because he has discovered how to say no or push his bowl away.

- If you feel your toddler is refusing to eat for **behavioural** reasons, manage the behaviour without getting into a power struggle.
  - Offer the refused food once more.
  - Offer an alternate food only once.
  - Tell your toddler that lunch will be over and show him a sign or some words to say – for example, "Thank you, no more".
  - Offer a small snack when you next would, but nothing for two hours before the next meal so that he has a good appetite for the next meal.
  - The next meal he will be hungry. You can rest assured: in 24 hours your toddler will have had enough calories.
- At around 18 months to three years old, your toddler will be asserting himself as he develops **autonomy** (a sense of being separate from you and having his own opinion). This is a vital stage and needs to be embraced – do not fight your toddler in the food arena. Give him his own bowl and spoon so he can feed himself. If you want to you can have a bowl for you to feed him too, but be sure he gets some control over his plate.
- Your toddler will develop his **own food preferences** and tastes. Always offer nutritious foods so that his options are limited to good food, not junk. Then let him choose within the boundaries of what you offer.
- Toddlers are often simply **too busy to eat**. Mealtimes should have the boundary of being seated at a table. Do not follow your toddler around with a plate of food. Feed him seated for each meal, with an interesting activity if necessary. A nice idea is to have an empty herb jar with some spaghetti sticks and have him post the spaghetti into the holes in the herb jar. Talk to him and sing with him. The idea is not to entertain and dance a jig to get him eating, but to take the focus off the task at hand and make meal times social.
- As soon as you can, have **family mealtimes**. Toddlers eat much better when part of an activity where others are doing the same. Social eating is a wonderful way to avert food refusal in toddlers.

Fussy eater and sensory difficulties

Sometimes a challenging feeder starts off as a challenging breast-feeder and continues to be a fussy eater, regardless of his stage of eating:

- In the early days these babies do not latch with ease and to get breast-feeding established may be a real nightmare, even with professional help
- If these babies do take to the breast eventually, they often won't shift off the breast and take bottles or dummies. They simply cannot tolerate the feel of latex or silicone in their mouths and mom's breast becomes not only a source of nutrition but also a pacifier.

- If they are bottle-fed, they will often only use one specific shape of teat, cannot tolerate fast flow and are easily thrown by a temperature change in the milk they are being offered.
- Their gag reflex does not diminish and introducing solids is a challenge.
- If these babies eat a jar of smooth fruit eventually, they simply will not move on to lumpy or stage two baby food.
- Homemade food with its tricky textures and different flavours is not accepted and these babies get 'stuck' on first stage jarred food or smooth cereals.
- As toddlers these little ones are notoriously bad eaters – they often develop fad eating and will only eat 'white' foods, for example yogurt, white bread, cheese and two-minute noodles. Meat is the most difficult food to tolerate.

If your baby has exhibited any or all of these symptoms and in addition is a high needs baby, you could well be looking at a sensory problem underlying his feeding difficulties.

SENSORY DEFENSIVENESS

A sensory defensive baby is not a happy chap. The sensory information in his environment, from smells, touch, tastes, sights, sound, movement and even the sensory information from his muscles and internal organs (interoception) is not filtered optimally and he is sensitive to every sensory input. This would be like spending all day at a busy baby expo – and we know how overwhelming all the sensory information at these events can be, even if we are processing sensory information normally. Babies with sensory defensiveness really battle with feeding for three main reasons:

OVERSTIMULATION

If your baby has sensory processing problems and the sensory input from his environment is not filtered out optimally, he will spend much of each day in an overstimulated state. Generally an overstimulated baby is oversensitive to new sounds and smells, cries at the drop of a hat and once crying is very difficult to sooth. Sensory defensive babies also do not sleep or eat well. You can imagine that it is very hard to eat if you are overstimulated, because you are feeling fractious. An overstimulated baby may be too distracted to latch on the breast, may arch his back when placed near the breast or laid in the horizontal feeding position. Coordinating suck, swallow and breathe when feeding is very difficult because he is not in the calm-alert state – the optimal state to feed.

You can try the following to help your over stimulated baby feed better:
- Watch his **awake times** very carefully – we know that overtiredness leads to overstimulation. If you keep your baby in a more settled routine and watch that he is not awake for too long, you will have more success with feeding.

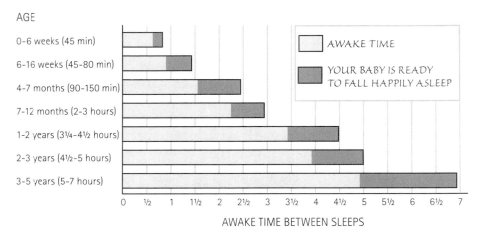

AGE

Age	
0-6 weeks (45 min)	
6-16 weeks (45-80 min)	
4-7 months (90-150 min)	
7-12 months (2-3 hours)	
1-2 years (3¼-4½ hours)	
2-3 years (4½-5 hours)	
3-5 years (5-7 hours)	

AWAKE TIME BETWEEN SLEEPS

- AWAKE TIME
- YOUR BABY IS READY TO FALL HAPPILY ASLEEP

From Sleep sense (Metz Press 2007)

- Feed **after sleeps** – after a sleep, your baby's sensory load is reset because his brain has had time to rest and process the sensory input from the last awake time. This means that he will more than likely be in the optimal state to feed.
- **Cover** your baby with a breast-feeding shawl or blanket while breast or bottle feeding if he is fussing at the breast. You may find that the quiet space is all he needs to feed better.
- Feed him in a **quiet space** if he is very distracted. This goes especially for toddlers who are too busy and overstimulated to sit still for long enough to eat.
- Do not feed your baby or toddler **in the kitchen** where there are likely to be smells that add to the levels of overstimulation.
- Place a **weighted blanket** (get one from an OT) or heavy pillow on your older baby or toddler's lap whilst in the high-chair. The deep pressure on his legs may settle him a bit.
- Some overstimulated babies and toddlers eat better after rocking or **rhythmic movement**. Rock your little baby until he is calm or take your toddler on a swing before mealtime.
- Change the **visual environment** to help you move your baby or toddler into a better state for eating. This could either be a quiet, stimulus free space or it may actually be watching TV. Many overstimulated toddlers settle into a calmer state if distracted by TV. Although this is not a great habit to encourage, it may be the only way to calm overstimulated toddler for feeding.
- With these babies, you do what you can to survive and help them eat. Take the pressure off yourself and if rules need to be bent, bend them.

ORAL DEFENSIVENESS

The touch receptors in your baby's mouth may be hypersensitive to touch. This will mean that touch, temperature and texture in your baby's mouth always feels new and novel. Instead of getting used to the feel of a nipple, teat, temperature, flavour or lump in mushy food, he will treat everything that goes into his mouth as a potential threat. Your baby's gag reflex remains very easily stimulated and he tends to gag on anything in his mouth. He may not even tolerate his hands in his mouth, so he will not mouth and suck on his hands as readily as another baby. This results in more fussing because he is unable to derive pleasure and self-calm by sucking. He may gag on dummies and most bottle teats and is therefore difficult to feed and to sooth. Oral defensiveness is best dealt with in consultation with a therapist – an OT or physiotherapist with experience in this area. They may employ the following techniques:

- Deep pressure **massage** inside your baby's mouth.
- If your baby will simply not tolerate the feel of your skin in his mouth and won't suck on your nipple, it is worth persisting with breast-feeding using a **nipple shield.**
- If you want to bottle feed and are battling to find a teat your baby will tolerate, try a **latex teat** as latex is often more readily tolerated. A 'Curity' teat is an old-fashioned shaped teat that many orally sensitive babies somehow tolerate better.
- Manage the **temperature** of food and milk with care – it is not worth upsetting the apple cart by serving food that is not the 'right' temperature for your sensitive baby.
- Try not to serve your sensitive baby jarred baby food – make your own at home from day one. Make his early food very smooth, as smooth as you can – you may need to add a little expressed breast or formula milk to get it smooth. You will never get the food as smooth as the jar food but this is a good thing because your baby may get 'stuck' on jar food and not tolerate **homemade** mush ever as it comes with lumps.
- If your baby gets stuck with a certain **texture** and always gags or vomits when offered food with that texture, just don't serve it until he is a little older. A good example is mashed potato with its unpredictable lumps.
- Some orally sensitive babies skip the mashed food phase altogether: They eat smooth, puréed food but then gag on lumpier mashed food, insisting on smooth food. Later – between 8 and 10 months of age – they may go straight onto soft, steamed **finger food**, which is predictable and they can control. These babies do better with baby-led weaning (see page 141).

TACTILE DEFENSIVENESS

Your baby may be fussy at mealtimes not because his mouth is sensitive but because his face and neck are sensitive to touch. We call this tactile defensiveness and it may manifest in combination with oral defensiveness and/or general sensory defensiveness. To limit the impact of tactile defensiveness at feeds:

- **Swaddle** your newborn for breast-feeds. The deep pressure of the swaddle plus the fact that the swaddling blanket prevents light touch from bothering your baby will improve the breast-feeding experience for him.
- Don't fiddle with your baby's face and head whilst feeding – don't stroke him – and later when he is eating in a high-chair, **don't wipe his face** if there is mush on his cheeks. Wiping his cheek may irritate him more than having a dirty face. Rather let him hold a damp facecloth and do it himself when he is old enough.

- Choose a **bib** of a texture your baby or toddler can manage. Take note when mealtimes go pear-shaped – it may be the fussing with tying a bib or the texture of the bib itself.

POOR WEIGHT GAIN

We live in a society obsessed with **weight** and it starts as early as that first weigh in at the clinic. Ask any mom what her baby's weight is and she will tell you to the last gram. Ask that same mom what her baby's head circumference is and she will give you a vague estimate or merely say, 'I'm not sure but it is all on track'. While monitoring your baby's weight is important, it is only a small part of the assessment to determine whether he is thriving. It is important to look at your baby and not the scale.

Sadly, many a mom has stopped breast-feeding because she was told that her baby's weight gain was not adequate, and yet her baby was healthy, eating well and meeting developmental milestones. Some babies simply are a lot smaller or larger than others. Bear this in mind if you are told that your baby does not have 'normal weight gain'. If someone were to ask you what a 38-year-old woman should weigh, you would laugh, as this is bound to vary according to height, ethnicity, genetics, bone structure and more. Yet babies are expected to fit onto charts that don't take feeding choices, genetics or almost anything else into consideration.

If you have been told that your baby's weight gain is inadequate, consider this list of questions:
- Is your baby keen to feed?
- Is he passing stools and urine regularly?
- Are his eyes bright and alert?
- Is his skin a healthy colour and texture?
- Is he moving his arms and legs vigorously?
- Are his nails growing?
- Is he meeting his developmental milestones?
- Is he alert when he is awake?

And then two more fundamental questions: How tall is Mom? How tall is Dad?

By answering all these questions, you will probably come to the conclusion that your baby is gaining weight adequately, without looking at his growth chart. Too many mothers and babies lose the breast-feeding experience because someone looked harder at the scale than the baby. Older babies, two to 12 months of age, grow at varying rates. Weight gain should not be used as the sole criterion for good health. Use other factors in addition to weight to determine your baby's overall health and well-being.

If your baby is not gaining weight at all or is losing weight, consult your doctor.

A growth chart is a useful tool to gauge general growth (see Appendix A for more information). You will be issued one at the birth of your baby. To make sensible use of a growth chart use it as follows:

- Always weigh your baby naked.
- Weigh your baby no more than once a week for the first six weeks and thereafter every two weeks until the age of 12 weeks.
- Always use the same scale.
- Do not look for grams of weight gain but general trends – is your baby consistently gaining or is his growth static or declining.
- Before becoming alarmed, weigh for three weeks in a row. If the trend is consistently static or there is a decline over three weeks, consult a healthcare professional.

Failure to thrive

Failure to thrive means that your baby is not growing as well as could be expected. There are various reasons for this. Some babies fail to grow because of repeated illness such as diarrhoea, pneumonia, genetic syndromes or cerebral palsy just to mention a few. Other babies don't gain weight as a result of not getting enough to eat.

When considering failure to thrive, it is important to bear in mind that your baby's pattern of growth over time is more important than individual measurements. For example, some dinky babies may be in the 25th percentile for height and weight on the growth chart, meaning that 75% of all babies of the same age are bigger than they are. If they continue growing on this curve, there is no cause for concern. However, if your baby was in the 75th percentile for weight and height, but suddenly loses weight and drops to the 25th percentile, further investigation is warranted.

MANAGING FAILURE TO THRIVE

If your baby has been diagnosed as 'failing to thrive', you need to find **professionals** who specialize in this area. A high-protein diet is not necessarily the key to weight gain. In fact, diets too high in protein can put a strain on young kidneys and be harmful to your baby's health. A dietician will help you assess the overall energy intake and assist you in increasing the energy and protein appropriately to meet your baby's extra needs. Depending on the cause of poor weight gain or weight loss, different recommendations will be offered:

- If your doctor suspects a physical cause for growth difficulty, special **medical tests** may be recommended and treatment required to resolve the problem.
- The solution could be as **simple** as switching formulas, or assessing for allergies.
- In some cases, failure to thrive may be related to **sucking and swallowing problems** and then a visit to an occupational or speech therapist specializing in feeding problems will be recommended.

OVERWEIGHT AND RAPID WEIGHT GAIN

Research indicates that babies who gain weight rapidly during the first six months may be more likely to become obese later in life. Although there are genetic and medical causes for overweight and rapid weight gain, by far the majority of overweight babies and children are overweight because of what they eat. If your baby's weight to height ratio indicates that he is gaining too much weight for his height, he may be overweight and you should have his intake assessed by a healthcare professional who will guide you on normalizing it.

There is much you can do to prevent overweight and obesity:

- Babies started on **solid foods** at too early an age could be at a greater risk for weight problems later in life. Babies started on solids before the age of two months have an increased risk of becoming obese adults.
- Compared with breast-fed babies, **formula-fed** (normal cow's milk or soya formula) babies have greater weight gain in infancy. This may put your baby at a greater risk of obesity later on in life. Cow's milk formula has a higher protein content than your breast milk and high protein intake in your baby's first year may increase the risk of adult obesity.
- If you are using a normal formula it is very important not to exceed the amounts recommended for your baby. Do not add **protein supplements** to feeds unless so advised by your healthcare practitioner.
- Babies who are **underweight** or **premature** have a risk of being fattened up and overfed in the first year of life and this puts them at a higher risk of obesity later in life. Make sure your baby is receiving sufficient energy and nutrients to meet his growing needs. As long as he is developing, healthy and thriving, you can continue feeding as you are – don't be tempted to '*make* your baby gain more weight'.

Managing overweight and weight gain

As a parent you can help prevent childhood obesity by providing healthy meals and snacks, daily physical activity, and nutrition education.

- For a younger baby, ensure that his **milk intake** does not exceed his daily requirements, especially once his solids intake becomes more significant.
- **Healthy meals and snacks** provide nutrition for growing bodies while modelling healthy eating behaviour and attitudes sets a good example.
- Watch your baby and toddler's **physical activity**. TV watching for older babies and toddlers should not exceed 30 minutes – they need to move and play.
- **Teaching** your little ones about healthy eating by showing them a healthy plateful of food helps them develop an awareness of good nutrition and healthy eating habits for a lifetime. You can start with nutrition education from a young age. Explore the food properties of a carrot with your baby while feeding her mashed carrots. Make food faces with fruit and vegetables and then explain how these foods keep your eyes, skin and hair healthy. These simple activities and conversations will all engender a healthy awareness of good nutrition.

PHYSICAL FEEDING DIFFICULTIES

Usually if your baby has a serious physical problem that will limit his ability to feed well, it will be diagnosed in the hospital and by the time you are discharged you will be equipped to cope with it or be seen weekly after discharge.

Cleft lip and palate

This is also referred to as a hair lip. The palate and/or upper lip does not close properly during development *in utero*, leaving a gap in the lip and a gap in the centre of the palate. This means that the mouth cavity is open to the nose cavity through the palate. This gap needs to be sealed properly in order for your baby to feed.

MANAGING A CLEFT LIP AND PALATE
- Do try to establish **breast-feeding**. Taking the breast with the nipple and areola right into the mouth seals the gap and may allow for good sucking.
- There are special soft **bottles** and long soft teats that can be used if breast-feeding is not possible or is unsuccessful.
- **Dentists** can make a plate to fit onto the palate that then blocks the hole and allows for feeding.
- Correction of the problem with **plastic surgery** is necessary and is usually performed after the first three months of life. Some of the more severe cleft palates require more than one operation.
- It is important to contact a **speech therapist** who has an interest in cleft lips early in the feeding process for advice and ongoing therapy or to contact the Cleft Palate Society (see page 173) for information and referral.

Tongue tie

The tongue is attached to the floor of the mouth by a band of tissue called the frenulum. If your baby's frenulum is shortened or if it is attached to the tongue very close to the tip of the tongue, he has a tongue tie. If the tip of your baby's tongue forms a groove and resembles the top of a heart shape when he tries to push his tongue over the lower gums, this indicates tongue tie. If the tongue tie is very tight, he will find it difficult to suck properly. It is common to see babies with a mild tongue tie.

MANAGING TONGUE TIE

This does not need any treatment. In fact, tongue tie almost always improves with time. As your baby grows and the jaw and tongue grow, so the apparent tongue tie improves. Your doctor may recommend having the frenulum clipped only if the tongue tie is very severe and interfering with feeding.

Low tone

If your baby has low tone, the muscles in a certain area of the body are a little lazy and don't respond to instruction from the brain as one would expect. Low tone around the mouth results in mushy muscles and poor eating and speech. This is because the tongue doesn't push the food around the mouth for chewing as it should and the muscles in the jaw, cheek and lips don't aid with chewing and swallowing optimally.

MANAGING LOW TONE
Seek the help of a speech therapist or occupational therapist specialized in feeding difficulties. Also try these ideas at home:
• Blowing bubbles (toddler and older)
• Sucking juice, frozen juices or even jelly through a straw (from seven months)
• Putting a blob of peanut butter (if your baby doesn't have peanut allergies) on the outer top lip or around the lips and showing him how to lick it off (from seven months).

Increased tone (spasticity)

A traumatic birth, especially if it involved oxygen deprivation or if your baby was born very premature, can result in increased tone and complicated feeding problems as the mouth simply does not work to keep food in or to chew and swallow. This is usually associated with general muscle tone problems such as increased tone. These problems must be addressed in therapy as other areas of the body, such as the neck stability and body control, may also be impacting on eating.

PERSONAL DIFFICULTIES

Like all areas of early parenting, be it sleep, calming your baby or feeding your baby, your relationship with your baby will impact his behaviour.

Ghosts in the kitchen

There may be something that you are not even aware of about the way you are managing your baby's feeding that is causing some difficulties. We call this subtle, invisible aspect of feeding 'ghosts in the kitchen' – something about your past and your attitude to feeding that is causing hassles for you and your baby. If you recognize a 'ghost' from the list below, it is worth seeking counselling to address any areas of difficulty:
• If you had a difficult **relationship with your mom** regarding the way you were fed or a loss that you feel about your relationship with her, you may have issues with feeding your baby. If you lost your mom early in life, you may fear losing your baby and in that way subconsciously prevent your toddler from moving on to independent feeding, for fear of losing him as a baby.

- You may find it very hard to read your **baby's signals**. His signals for hunger, fullness and when he wants the next mouthful, for instance. You may also misread his signals and feel that he is rejecting you whilst breast-feeding when he is actually just a little overstimulated or uncomfortable. Reading feeding signals is challenging, so spend time on this aspect of feeding.
- You may have a hard time dealing with your toddler's need for **autonomy and separation**. Toddlers are at a stage in their life when they fight to be independent. This is particularly so when it comes to feeding. Try not to fight your toddler's need to control what he eats and to feed himself, even if it results in an almighty mess.

Your sensory defensiveness

When things go wrong with breast-feeding, you will experience significant feelings of guilt. You may be told that if you feel pain you have the latch wrong. You may also be told that letdown is not supposed to be painful. You will feel guilty for not loving this 'natural' experience. It is important to realize that every mom and baby are different and bring a different sensory experience to the feeding relationship. If breast-feeding is going wrong, it may simply be a sensory issue for you and/or your baby.

MANAGING SENSORY DEFENSIVENESS

If you are a sensory sensitive person and in addition find that the experience of being a new mom stressful, you may be even more sensitive at feed times. If you find breast-feeding painful or don't enjoy the sensation, it is worth looking at the way you process sensory information and some suggestions to help you manage your sensory experience of feeding:
- **Sleep** in the afternoons as sleep will help your sensory system to reset so that you can cope better with the sensory input of feeding, particularly in the late afternoon.
- Feed in **quiet spaces** so that the sensory input of feeding is all you have to cope with and you have less chance of becoming overloaded.
- Place a **warmed heavy pillow** filled with barley and lavender (available at most pharmacies) around your neck to help you relax while you feed.
- Play gentle, **soothing music** to help regulate your state and make you feel calm and therefore tolerate the touch experience of feeding better.

Feeding is probably the most emotionally fraught aspect of parenting. When it goes wrong, it creates anxiety and distress for all. If you have identified areas in this chapter where you know you or your baby are having difficulty, it is really worth addressing them with the help of a professional: paediatrician, dietician, occupational therapist or physiotherapist, psychologist or your well-baby nurse.

Allergies

Charmaine had battled with allergies her entire life. She had itchy eczema every winter and her hay fever led to an asthma attack almost every year. Now that she was having her first baby she wanted to make sure the baby was less allergic. Even though she was not allergic to any foods, she wondered about her diet in pregnancy and whether avoiding or consuming specific foods would prevent or cause allergies in her baby. She was also not sure about the right time to introduce solids and what she should avoid giving her baby to reduce her risk of allergies.

There is a good chance that you know at least one person with an allergic child. While it is true that allergies are on the increase, it is also a fact that allergies are over-diagnosed and that many a little one is having a very limited diet on the mere suspicion of allergies. The term *allergy* is used so randomly nowadays that it is easy to end up confused and misled over what can prevent allergies and how to manage them.

So let's look at the facts.

WHAT IS AN ALLERGY?

An allergy is a specific reaction of your immune system to a protein. The protein as such is not harmful to the body, but is interpreted by the body as foreign or not belonging to it. This triggers your immune system to create antibodies to this protein – effectively calling cells to action to defend the body. The antibody thus produced triggers the allergic reaction by releasing chemicals such as histamine. The first symptoms of an allergic reaction occur within minutes of swallowing the food and include skin rashes or swelling, vomiting and cramps, flares of eczema, asthma or a runny, itchy, sneezy nose and itchy eyes. A delayed reaction may occur hours to a day or two later and includes tummy pains, vomiting, nausea and eczema.

NOT AN ALLERGY

Alice's little girl was three weeks early and was delivered by caesarean section. By six weeks old, she was gaining weight wonderfully but she was a very irritable baby who really battled with gas and bowel discomfort. She seemed to react to breast milk and Alice was told by a friend who had a similar problem that her baby was probably allergic to breast milk and that she should put her on a lactose-free formula.

It is extremely unlikely that your baby will be allergic to your breast milk. In very rare circumstances your baby may react to an allergen you are ingesting that is transmitted through your breast milk. If anybody tells you that your baby is allergic, get a second opinion as many of the so-called allergic reactions to food

are in fact not allergies at all. Your baby's reactions may well look just like an allergy but may be due to a number of other causes you should consider:

Lactose intolerance

Enzyme deficiencies lead to intolerance to foods such as dairy or fruit. It is important to distinguish between lactose intolerance and allergy. Lactose is a sugar naturally found in most milk and milk products including breast milk, all cow's milk based baby feeding formulas and all dairy products, including cow's milk, goat's milk, yogurt and cheese.

Lactose is digested in your baby's stomach by an enzyme called lactase. If your baby has no lactase enzyme or the lactase enzyme is temporarily disrupted, she will become lactose intolerant.

NORMAL LACTOSE INTOLERANCE IN NEWBORNS

Like all babies in the first few months of life, Alice's baby has a degree of lactose intolerance. This is probably because the amount of lactose that she ingests daily in milk is more than the lactase enzyme in her gut can digest in a day. In a breast-fed baby, this is indicated by a yellow and loose stool. If your baby is under six months of age and has some discomfort from gas and explosive stools, she may have a degree of lactose intolerance that she will outgrow as her lactase enzymes increase over time. Do not be tempted to stop breast-feeding or put your baby on lactose-free formula at this stage.

LACTOSE INTOLERANCE AFTER GASTRO

Lactose intolerance can also occur after a bout of diarrhoea and vomiting. Severe diarrhoea causes thinning of the lining of the intestine and the lactase enzyme is temporarily lost. Stopping dairy and using a lactose-free formula for about two weeks allow the intestine to recover and the lactose intolerance will disappear. There is no need to stop breast-feeding unless the intolerance is severe.

CONTINUED LACTOSE INTOLERANCE

If your baby has severe, ongoing lactose intolerance she will be very uncomfortable with a lot of gas and wind in a bloated abdomen, very watery, explosive, frothy stools and will not be growing well. This all settles down within days of removing lactose from the diet.

BOTTLE AND BREAST-FEEDING

Lactose intolerance in the first three months of life is usually mild and there is no need to stop breast-feeding. Babies who are not growing well, cramping terribly and have diagnosed lactose intolerance with a complete absence of lactase enzyme may do better off the breast. If a stool test strongly indicates lactose intolerance it is okay to stop breast-feeding for a few days to see if there is a definite improvement.

Lactose-free formulas are available for bottle feeding and include soya formulas and lactose-free cow's milk formulas.

Only the most severe forms of lactose intolerance will continue when your baby is ready to start solids. All dairy products contain lactose so you will need to avoid cow's milk, goat's milk, ice cream, chocolate, yogurt and cheese.

Lactose intolerance usually settles within the first six months of life. True congenital deficiency of the lactase enzyme causing life-long lactose intolerance is exceptionally rare.

Food poisoning

If your baby is sick after eating meat, chicken or fish, you will wonder if she is allergic to the food. You need to bear in mind that if the meat is off or contaminated with a parasite, it will make your baby sick. If meat, chicken or fish is not kept cold it can be infected with bacteria, which will make your baby very sick with food poisoning within a few hours of eating the food.

Always be extra cautious with meat, chicken and fish, ensuring that you use fresh produce, properly stored and thoroughly cooked when preparing your own baby food.

Food aversion

Obviously we don't all like the same food and some of us have a real dislike for specific foods or tastes. Your baby or toddler may have an intense dislike for a particular food and avoid it by gagging or vomiting whenever you feed it to her. This is the only signal she can give – to spit out the food or avoid it – and in the absence of any other symptoms should not be mistaken for an allergy.

Coincidental reaction while ingesting food

If your baby vomits after a feed, it may be due to something completely other than an allergic reaction. Your baby or toddler may be gagging on the food and end up vomiting, or may be developing gastroenteritis, which is causing the vomiting. Offer the food at another time before assuming that your baby is allergic.

Food additives

While it is possible to react to any of the colourants and preservatives in food, it is very rare for them to produce a true allergic reaction.

The sulphur preservatives frequently cause reactions. Sulphur dioxide is used in fruit products – dried fruit, concentrated fruit juices and fruit flavoured mixing drinks. It causes a tight chest in susceptible children and can cause acute asthma. This is the preservative that makes our throat itch when we drink fruit juice.

Sodium benzoate, monosodium glutamate (MSG), tartrazine and any other of the common colourants and preservatives can cause abdominal upsets or skin reactions.

SENSE-ABLE FEEDING
Lactose is altered in the process of making yogurt, cottage cheese and hard cheese, and is usually less of a problem in these products.

SENSE-ABLE FEEDING
Do not assume that your baby is allergic to fish if it makes her ill. She may well be reacting to the fish being off or to a parasite in the fish, which may mimic an allergic reaction. The best thing to do is to have an allergy test for the fish that you thought caused the reaction. If the test is negative then your baby is not allergic to that type of fish.

SENSE-ABLE FEEDING
If you do not prepare home-made food for your baby, stick to baby food that contains no added preservatives and colourants.

While any food may cause an allergic reaction, these are the most common allergens:

- Milk
- Soya
- Egg
- Wheat
- Fish
- Peanuts

Typical allergic reactions

An allergic reaction to these foods will cause any one or more of the following symptoms:

- *Skin reactions*: eczema, hives, swelling of the lips and/or throat.
- *Gastrointestinal reactions*: nausea, vomiting, cramps and tummy pains, occasionally diarrhoea, and babies may present with colic.
- *Nose*: hay fever (allergic rhinitis) causes sneezing and an itchy, runny and blocked nose.
- *Eyes*: itchy, red and watery eyes.
- *Chest*: asthma, ongoing coughing and wheezing at night, triggered by exposure to allergens in the air.
- *Anaphylaxis*: a life-threatening reaction causing a drop in blood pressure, shortness of breath or stopping breathing, necessitating emergency life-saving treatment with adrenaline. This reaction is rare.

Asthma and hay fever are uncommon reactions to foods and are unlikely to be the only reaction. Usually a baby or toddler will develop eczema as the first sign of allergies to food and then as the baby grows up and develops other allergies, hay fever or asthma can develop.

CAN YOU PREVENT FOOD ALLERGIES?

It would be ideal if you could prevent your baby from developing allergies, especially if you have allergies. Theories on this topic abound, often not backed by scientific evidence. It is worth considering the following research-based information in your quest to prevent allergies.

Pregnancy and breast-feeding

Allergens like proteins in milk, egg and peanuts can be transferred to your baby in tiny amounts in breast milk. Even during pregnancy, your unborn baby's immune system can react by producing antibodies to allergenic proteins. Nevertheless, there is no evidence that avoiding allergenic foods either during pregnancy or while breast-feeding will prevent allergies in your baby. In fact, the opposite may be true.

You should eat an inclusive diet, with the exception of foods you are allergic to, both during pregnancy and while breast-feeding. Do not restrict any other foods, including dairy, eggs and peanuts – restricting these foods will not prevent allergies in your baby, whereas eating them may actually improve her tolerance and reduce her chances of developing an allergy.

The truth is that there is no dietary intervention that prevents all allergies. Exclusive breast-feeding for the first four months of life has a minor effect on preventing or delaying the occurrence of eczema, but this is only true for your baby if you or your baby's dad have allergies, and specifically eczema. There is no definite evidence that exclusive breast-feeding reduces eczema or any other allergy if there is no history of the allergy in Mom or Dad.

Formula feeding

If you are not able to exclusively breast-feed **and** there is a history of allergies in Mom or Dad, you should use an extensively hydrolysed cow's milk formula. The effect will possibly be the delayed onset of eczema but there will be no effect on asthma, food allergies or hay fever.

Starting solids

Starting solids too early can lead to an increase in food allergies and intolerances. This is true. The question is, "When is too early?"

Starting solids before four months (17 weeks) of age will potentially increase the risk of food allergies. There seems to be a window of opportunity for starting solids between four and six months of age, which will potentially decrease eczema, food allergies and possibly wheezing in the first three years of life in children at risk for allergies. There is no hard and fast rule that you have to start with cereals or fruit or vegetables. It is clear that none of these causes harm so give what you feel is right.

Avoiding or delaying foods

If you follow our advice on the introduction of solids, you will see that it is done systematically during the first nine months. You may have been advised to avoid allergenic foods such as peanuts, eggs and fish so as to prevent food reactions. But there is no evidence that avoiding these foods actually has any benefit in the long run. There is also no need to delay introducing any foods beyond six months of age in the hope that this will prevent allergies. If your baby is going to be allergic to egg, she will be allergic whether it is offered at six months or at 18 months.

DIAGNOSING FOOD ALLERGIES

When worrying about food allergies, it is important to be sensible. Few babies and children have true allergies to food and it is worth seeking the advice of a qualified doctor rather than self-diagnosing such a problem. Diagnosing a food allergy is not always easy but nonetheless it is very important to be sure that a food is in fact responsible for a reaction before eliminating it from you baby's diet.

For mild reactions like hay fever and eczema, you may well try eliminating the suspected food for a time to see if the allergy symptoms disappear. Then the food should be reintroduced to see if the symptoms return. Once you reintroduce the food, you can determine if it is in fact causing or aggravating the symptoms.

If your baby persistently has the following symptoms, it is worth seeing your doctor to check for allergies:

- Eczema (persistent skin rashes or dry patches)
- Asthma
- Hay fever
- Gastrointestinal upsets like nausea, vomiting and cramping.

When you go to your doctor he may refer you to a specialist or do allergy screening that may include any of the following:

- Talking to you about your family and your baby to try to work out what food could be causing the reaction. This is often much more important than actually doing the tests.
- Screening test (Fx5 Food Screen) – this screens for sensitivity to egg, fish, soya, milk, peanuts and wheat. It will indicate if your baby needs to have a RAST or skin prick test.
- Skin-prick testing – a tiny amount of a substance containing the allergen you want to test for, such as egg, is introduced into a prick on the skin and you will watch for a reaction like a mosquito bite for 10 minutes. The severity of the reaction indicates whether your baby is allergic.
- Blood tests for specific antibodies (RAST tests) – your baby's blood will be drawn and a test will measure the allergic response to certain foods. This is an expensive test but is good for just about everything we eat.
- CAST testing – a blood test used for the common food allergens, but most often used to detect possible allergy to colourants, preservatives and drugs.

If the allergy test is negative, you can be certain that your baby is not allergic. A positive test does not absolutely prove that the food tested was the cause of the reaction. Your doctor will determine this based on other information in conjunction with the test. If the test is strongly positive, you can be almost certain that the reaction was due to the specific food.

If your baby is diagnosed as allergic, you will be told to avoid the food and consult a dietician.

MISDIAGNOSIS OF ALLERGIES

Misdiagnosing or overdiagnosing food allergies leads to potential problems:
- You could end up eliminating foods that are not actually causing any harm.
- You could be eliminating foods that are essential for good nutrition and it may be a challenge to find substitutes.
- You may end up avoiding the wrong food and cause an allergic reaction by offering your baby something that you think is safe

MANAGING FOOD ALLERGIES

Food allergies are not all that common in the general population, and the section below on managing allergies must only be considered after a confirmed diagnosis by a qualified professional.

Avoiding the food

The food that causes the allergy should be avoided in all its forms, especially if the reaction is very severe. Check the labels on products (which may be confusing) and ask restaurants about their food preparation and ingredients (for older children). You need to be vigilant at parties when children are eating sweets and cakes. This is easier said than done because your toddler will not know that the food should be avoided and often the allergen may be disguised in another form, for example eggs in sweets and cakes.

MIXED FOODS MASKING THE TRUE ALLERGEN

If your baby is eating a slice of cake and has a reaction, you may assume that she reacted to either the egg or the milk, because these are the most common allergens. Sometimes the reaction is not to the obvious ingredients but to something else. A cake may have traces of peanuts that you were unaware of and the reaction may actually be due to that. It is therefore very important to be accurate in your observations and conclusions when recalling events around an allergic reaction.

Cow's milk allergy

An allergic reaction to milk can range from skin rashes, diarrhoea and vomiting to anaphylaxis (although the last mentioned is extremely rare). All these reactions can be mild or serious. The good news is that most children outgrow their cow's milk allergy by three to five years of age. In the meantime, if you are going to cut cow's milk from your baby's diet, the question becomes what other milk options you should explore.

SOYA

If your baby develops an allergy to cow's milk you will probably be advised to try a soy formula. It is important to know that there is an overlap in cow's milk and soya allergies. If the reaction to the cow's milk is mild (e.g. eczema), there should be no problem trying the soya formula, bearing in mind that about 15 per cent of children will also react to soya. If your baby has a severe reaction to cow's milk such as anaphylaxis or severe diarrhoea and vomiting, she has a 30 per cent chance of being allergic to soya too.

HYDROLYSED HYPOALLERGENIC (HA) COW'S MILK FORMULAS

These are not suitable for children with cow's milk allergy. The formulas still contain cow's milk protein and an allergic child will react to them. Remember, an allergic reaction has nothing to do with lactose, so lactose-free formulas are just as bad for babies with cow's milk allergy.

GOAT'S MILK

It is not an option and should not be used for children at all. Children allergic to cow's milk may also be allergic to goat's milk because the proteins are so similar. In addition, goat's milk is deficient in vitamin C and folate, and has a high level of sodium, which can lead to kidney problems and dehydration.

AMINO ACID OR ELEMENTAL FORMULAS

These are the only milk formulas suitable for children with cow's milk allergy. After the first year of life it is acceptable to use rice milk along with a calcium supplement, provided your child is eating a well-balanced diet.

COW'S MILK ALLERGY: FOODS TO AVOID

In case of cow's milk allergy, remember to exclude cow's milk in all forms and look for these items on food labels:
- Chocolate, ice cream, yoghurt, custard
- Butter, margarine
- Whey, casein, cream
- Milk solids
- Any ingredient that starts with *lacto-*

Egg allergy

If your baby is allergic to egg, she can have any of the symptoms previously mentioned. Most little ones who are allergic to egg will outgrow the allergy by about five years of age. Until then, avoid egg and any product made with eggs.

EGG ALLERGY: FOODS TO AVOID

Read the labels on food and look out for these:
- Albumin
- Dried egg
- Egg white, yolk
- Egg solids, substitutes, powder
- Globulin
- Lecithin, livetin, lysozyme
- Vitellin
- Ovalbumin
- Any ingredient that starts with *ovo-*

VACCINATIONS AND EGG ALLERGY

The measles and MMR (measles, mumps and rubella) vaccines are not cultured in chicken eggs but on the skin cells of chicks. Administering these vaccines therefore holds no risk in case of egg allergy. Flu vaccine and yellow fever vaccine, however, are cultured in chicken eggs and it is important that children who are allergic to eggs only receive these vaccines under strict medical supervision.

Peanut allergy

A peanut allergy is potentially serious as it can lead to severe reactions. If your baby has asthma together with a peanut allergy, she is at risk of anaphylactic episodes as she grows up. Unfortunately she won't outgrow a peanut allergy, but it does not mean that she is allergic to all nuts. Each type of nut needs to be tested individually if a reaction has occurred and you don't know which nut caused it.

<table>
<tr><td>PEANUT ALLERGY: FOODS TO AVOID</td><td>When avoiding peanuts also check labels for:
• Peanut oil
• Mixed nuts
• Arachis oils
• Products manufactured in a factory where peanuts are processed</td></tr>
</table>

If your baby or toddler is severely allergic to peanuts, you need carry an adrenaline syringe and make sure there is one available at her crèche and at home. It is important to ask your doctor about this syringe and how to use it. Always ensure that your syringes have not passed their expiry date.

Wheat allergy

Non-allergic reactions to wheat in the form of abdominal cramps and vomiting are far more common than true allergic reactions. One example of a non-allergic condition is celiac disease (severe gluten intolerance), which causes malabsorption of nutrients, diarrhoea and failure to thrive. The role of wheat in eczema and asthma is greatly overemphasised, so be sure that the allergy is correctly diagnosed otherwise your baby will end up on a wheat restricted diet for no real reason nor benefit.

<table>
<tr><td>WHEAT ALLERGY: FOODS TO AVOID</td><td>When avoiding wheat also check labels for:
• Bran, edible starch
• Cereal extract
• Couscous
• Cracker meal
• Gluten, gluten flour
• Durum wheat
• Semolina wheat
• Anything mentioning wheat e.g. wheat germ
• Hydrolyzed vegetable flour</td></tr>
</table>

Too sick to eat?

CHAPTER 7

Daniel had a tough start in life. Even though he was a full-term baby he spent his first four weeks in the neonatal ICU and very nearly lost his life. Understandably his mom was very sensitive to changes in his health. He suffered repeated bouts of bronchitis and severe diarrhoea landed him back in hospital at six months of age. It seemed as soon as he was settling into a good sleeping and eating routine, his health would go out the window and set him back. His mom knew whenever he was getting sick because he would stop eating a day before the symptoms occurred. Then, once well, he would take ages to start eating properly again. He was a small baby and his growth curve resembled a rocky road with lots of ups and downs.

When a baby stops eating or drinking and becomes listless or very irritable, the first thought to pop into any rational parent's head is, "Is my baby too sick to eat?" Even as adults, we lose our appetite when we are sick, because the last thing you feel like doing when you are sick is eating. Likewise, even babies who eat and drink well when healthy will not want to eat and will fuss a lot when feeling unwell. If the illness is short-lived, your baby may well lose a little bit of weight but will certainly regain his appetite and weight very quickly once fully recovered.

FEVER

A high fever refers to a body temperature above 39°C measured in the ear or bottom and above 38.5°C measured under the arm.

A fever is not an illness and is also not dangerous, it is a normal response of a healthy immune system to an infection. It leads to rapid breathing and causes a fast heartbeat. High fevers do not have a lasting negative effect and even if your baby has a fever fit or convulsion, the fit is not harmful unless he has an existing neurological problem.

Effect on feeding

A fever may well result in less drinking and reduced or loss of appetite.

What to do

Bring the fever down to make your baby feel better. It is appropriate when the fever is over 39°C to give your baby Paracetamol or Ibuprofen at the recommended dose. You can also undress him and sponge his face and forehead with a damp cloth. Do not use cold baths or wrap your baby in cold sheets or towels. This will make your baby very distressed and cause him to shiver, which will raise his body temperature.

> Your baby may stop eating/drinking as a result of
> - Fever
> - Blocked nose/nasal congestion
> - A common cold
> - Croup
> - Sinusitis
> - Hay fever
> - Pneumonia
> - Bronchiolitis
> - Ear infections
> - Sore throat or mouth
> - Nausea and vomiting
> - Tummy pain

Give your baby lots to drink. A fever causes fluid loss through perspiration and rapid breathing. In addition, your baby will not want to feed or drink, therefore not compensating naturally for the fluids lost. It is important therefore to make sure that he is drinking at least 60% of what he normally does.

When to call the doctor

A fever on its own is not a problem and as long as there are no other symptoms it is generally safe to watch and control a fever for 48 hours. A fever that persists beyond this time is a reason to see a doctor. Any baby under three months of age with a high fever must be seen by a doctor as an emergency.

Your baby should be seen by a doctor if he has a fever accompanied by any of the following symptoms:

- Coughing and rapid breathing
- Diarrhoea
- Headache and stiff neck
- Bites on the skin
- Vomiting
- Skin rashes
- Travel to malaria areas
- Pain anywhere

BLOCKED NOSE/NASAL CONGESTION

From birth, babies only breathe through their nose. Therefore, it is obviously important that your baby's nose is clear so that he can breathe whilst feeding. Healthy babies often get a blocked nose in the first few months of life. Living in air-conditioned homes or polluted city environments or high grass pollen areas all play a role in producing nasal mucus. This mucus sits in your new baby's tiny nasal passages and a small bit of mucus will cause what sounds like a big blockage.

Effect on feeding

If your baby's nose is very congested you may find that he battles to breathe while feeding.

What to do

> **SENSE-ABLE FEEDING**
> Just because your baby has a blocked nose does not mean that he has allergies or needs to change formula.

You will probably be more worried by the sound of the blocked nose than your baby is. The best thing you can do is to flush the nose with sterile salt water (saline) to soften the mucus and help the nose to clear. The saline has no magical medicinal property – it works by flushing the mucus through the nose and then into the throat where it is swallowed. One drop in each nostril may not do the trick – use enough of the solution to be sure that the nose is properly cleared.

When to call the doctor

It is not necessary to call the doctor for simple nasal congestion without a fever.

THE COMMON COLD

The most common upper respiratory tract infection (URTI) is the common cold. It is caused by a virus and leads to a watery, runny nose for about three days, which then becomes blocked with yellow mucus. At this stage there may be a low grade fever. The fever and blocked nose last about three days and then your baby may well start to cough. The cough is phlegmy and worse at night and lasts about five days. So the condition lasts seven to ten days.

Effect on feeding

Children usually don't feed or drink well when they have a cold, so it is important to pay attention to keeping your baby's nose clear so that he can suck and drink. Offer smaller amounts of liquids frequently.

What to do

There is no specific therapy, but keeping the nose clear by flushing it with saline and then putting decongestant nose drops into the nose will help to alleviate the symptoms. Antibiotics are **not** needed to treat a common cold because the cold is caused by a virus. Antibiotics only treat bacterial infections.

When to call the doctor

The following symptoms may indicate that your baby has something other than a common cold and needs to be seen by a doctor:
- A fever of more than 38.5°C lasting for more than 2 days
- Poor feeding when the nose is clear
- Vomiting or diarrhoea
- Difficulty breathing and rapid breathing
- Noisy breathing: grunting, whistling or wheezing
- Overly sleepy or listless

CROUP

Croup is a viral infection that causes swelling of the windpipe in the area of the vocal cords, which results in noisy breathing and a barking cough. The typical cough is described as sounding like the bark of a seal. The condition can start with a wet 'snotty nose' for a few days, followed by the noisy breathing, or it can start very suddenly usually between 22h00 and 02h00. Your baby may go to bed seemingly completely well and then wake with a deep barking cough. Noisy breathing heard on both breathing in and breathing out is called stridor and is the worrying sign in croup.

What to do

Keep your baby calm and quiet. If your baby has a fever, treat it and ensure that he is drinking. Try steaming the air or go outside into the cold night air – very often one of these suggestions settles the croup quickly.

When to call the doctor

If your baby has a barking cough, is agitated and rasping when he breathes both in and out, he should be taken to the nearest emergency room.

SINUSITIS

Sinusitis is a blocked nose with thick mucus that lasts for more than seven days and is usually accompanied by a fever. This occurs because the drainage tubes from the sinuses are blocked by the congested nose. If the nose is blocked, the sinuses will be blocked and the normal mucus produced in the nose and sinuses does not drain properly. The fluid collects in the sinuses and leads to congestion, pain in the face, a blocked nose, fever and infection.

Effect on feeding

Aside from not being able to breathe while feeding, your baby will also have a loss of appetite owing to the fever and generally feeling unwell.

What to do

Clear the congestion by flushing the nose with saline and then use nasal drops or spray that contain cortisone (on prescription from your doctor). Antibiotics are necessary if there is fever and pain.

When to call the doctor

If your child is still sick after 48 hours on treatment or if his eyes and the eyelids start to become puffy and red it, is necessary to see the doctor again.

HAY FEVER

Hay fever is correctly known as *allergic rhinitis*, an allergic condition that causes:

- Itchy nose and eyes
- Sneezing
- Watery, runny nose
- Blocked nose

The sneezy, runny itchy nose happens quickly when we are exposed to an allergen such as grass or cats or dogs. The nasal blockage and thick discharge follow a few hours later. It is important to note that there is no fever and no feeling of being acutely ill. If the condition is not diagnosed and treated properly, it leads to chronic blockage of the nose and causes:

- Poor sleeping
- Snoring
- Feelings of tiredness and lethargy
- Loss of appetite and poor feeding
- Frequent ear infections or sinusitis

Chronic nasal blockage and sinus congestion cause specific features on the face:

- Dark rings under the eyes
- Mouth breathing

- Lines on the lower eyelid
- Upwards rubbing of the nose (nasal salute)
- High arched palate
- A line across the top of the nose (nasal crease)

What to do

Allergic rhinitis is generally very easily treated by:
- Identifying the allergy either from the history of knowing that the symptoms are worst when around cats or dogs or grass, or by performing specific allergy tests.
- Administering safe nose drops or nasal sprays that contain cortisone. These medications are safe and do not contain the harmful cortisones (steroids) you read about. These medications are regarded as controlling medications and should be used for long periods of time.
- Using antihistamines for the acute symptoms. The antihistamines must be the new generation antihistamines that do not cause drowsiness. Please check this with your doctor or pharmacist.

When to call the doctor

There are several different combinations of medication to treat this so if the medication is not working, call your doctor.

PNEUMONIA

This is a lower respiratory tract infection (LRTI) caused by either viruses or bacteria and affects the lung tissue, resulting in swelling and mucus production. This leads to rapid breathing with shortness of breath and fever. We have vaccines available as part of the recommended government schedule, which protect against the bacteria that cause pneumonia.

Effect on feeding

A baby with severe pneumonia will not eat or drink. In mild cases of pneumonia children manage to eat and drink.

What to do

Watch your baby closely to ensure that his fluid intake is adequate, that he does not require oxygen and that his breathing is not too fast and laboured. The treatment is with antibiotics and recovery is very quick.

When to call the doctor

Fever, rapid breathing and coughing are the warning signs of pneumonia. Watch your baby's breathing pattern and if the ribs are sucked in with the in breath or if you sense that your baby is struggling to breathe, see the doctor.

BRONCHIOLITIS

Bronchiolitis is a viral infection of the small airways of young children and is characterised by a blocked nose, wheezing and coughing. The virus that typically causes bronchiolitis is prevalent every year in autumn and winter. It produces huge amounts of mucus in the nose and the chest and this leads to difficulty breathing.

The infection starts as a snotty nose for about three days and this goes on to coughing, wheezing and rapid breathing. Take care when the wheezing starts because it usually gets worse over the next four days before it starts to get better. About one in ten babies under the age of one will require admission to hospital for observation and treatment during the acute phase of the illness. This means that the majority of children will cough and wheeze for about ten days but will cope with the illness. They are generally happy, not distressed and able to feed as long as their nose is kept clean, allowing them to breathe. Remember that young children prefer to breathe through their nose and find it really hard to breathe through the mouth.

Effect on feeding

Feeding is difficult for children with bronchiolitis because the nose is badly blocked. Don't worry about your baby not eating food, but ensure fluid intake even if it means using a syringe to get the fluid into the mouth. In severe cases children need to be hospitalized for intravenous fluids.

What to do

This infection gets better in its own time and there is nothing that will speed up the natural course of events. Manage bronchiolitis as follows to make your baby more comfortable:

- Treat any fever present.
- Make sure your baby's nose is clear of mucus by flushing with saline.
- Make sure that your baby's nappy is clean and dry, he is warm and is taking sufficient fluids. This will be taken in smaller amounts than usual and more frequently than usual.
- Medication does not help this condition. Many parents have nebulisers at home to use just in case their child has this kind of problem. Unfortunately nebulisation does not help the tight chest of a bronchiolitic. It may well help the very blocked-up nose but this is just as easily treated with saline nose drops or spray.

When to call the doctor

Danger signs of bronchiolitis, indicating the need for medical intervention, are:

- Children under 3 months of age
- Rapid breathing
- Poor feeding
- High fever
- Difficulty breathing
- Blue lips and tongue

EAR INFECTIONS

The ears are connected to the nose by tiny tubes (eustachian tubes) that let air up into the ear and this ensures that the ears work normally. If the nose is very blocked, the opening of these tubes will also be blocked; this will cause pressure changes in the ears and an infection may follow. The eardrum will become red and swollen from the infection and your baby will have a high fever and earache. Ear infections can also cause vomiting and diarrhoea, and your baby's sleep will become disrupted.

Effect on feeding

Sucking can be very painful when the ears are infected so your baby will feed poorly and cry when sucking.

What to do

The ear infection often improves without treatment in about two days, so control the pain and fever and flush the nose with saline. See your doctor if the pain and fever have not settled in two days, as your baby will probably need an antibiotic for the infection.

When to call the doctor

Call your doctor if:
- the fever and pain have not improved after two days on antibiotics
- yellow sticky fluid starts leaking out of your baby's ear
- your baby's ear starts to swell

SORE THROAT

A sore throat may indicate laryngitis or tonsillitis. Laryngitis is a viral infection that causes a hoarse voice and harsh cough. The cough is quite painful and the voice is soft. The infection only lasts a few days and gets better without treatment.

Tonsillitis is a very common illness and is caused by either viruses or bacteria. Our tonsils are found in the back of the soft palate on either side just beyond the uvula. They tonsils are an important part of the immune system in the first few years of life, but have no real purpose after the age of about four. Babies and children with tonsillitis have high fever and a sore throat. The throat is red and the tonsils are swollen and have yellow infected areas on them.

Effect on feeding

Owing to the sore throat your baby will not be interested in feeding or drinking, and may cry whenever he has to swallow.

What to do

You can't tell just by looking at the throat whether the tonsillitis was caused by a virus or is bacterial, but we know that tonsillitis in little ones under two is almost

TEETHING

Children get 20 teeth between the ages of six months and 30 months. Teething is blamed for everything from high fevers to poor feeding, poor sleeping, runny tummies and everything else. But teething is really not as big a deal as it is often made out to be. In fact, the best advice on teething is to ignore the process completely and delete the word from your brain as a possible cause of illness. *Teething causes teeth.*

Sure, children will get sick and have fevers and runny tummies between six and 30 months of age, but just because this is also the time that they are teething, it does not mean that the condition is caused by teething. Your baby may get sick because he is putting everything into his mouth and we know that we pick up bugs by transferring them via our hands to our mouths.

Effect on feeding

Teething has little effect on feeding. Occasionally more sensitive babies become fussy eaters for about a day or so around the eruption of a tooth.

What to do

Teething powders and gels numb the gums for a short time, perhaps 15 minutes, and have no effect on helping the teeth come out more quickly or more easily.

If your baby is sick at the same time that he is teething, do not just put the symptoms down to teething.

When to call the doctor

There is no need to call the doctor if your baby is simply teething. If your child is sick at the same time that he is teething, call the doctor if the symptoms do not get better because this means that the infection is getting worse. It is not the teething.

GASTROENTERITIS

Gastroenteritis (gastro) is a viral infection of the stomach and small intestine that leads to excessive vomiting and diarrhoea. After a few hours of vomiting your baby will develop very watery diarrhoea and this occurs more than three times a day. The vomiting usually lasts about 24 hours but the diarrhoea can last for up to seven days. The most common cause is the rotavirus and we have a very safe and effective vaccine against this, available as part of the government funded vaccines in South Africa.

Effect on feeding

If your baby has gastro he will feel nauseous and may have stomach cramps, both of which will cause loss of appetite. After the gastro has settled your baby may be lactose intolerant.

What to do

Don't worry about eating, but make sure he is drinking. Dehydration is the major complication you want to avoid and this is done by providing oral rehydration solution (ORS). This is a fluid made of salt, water and glucose and is rapidly absorbed after drinking. There are many commercially available ORS brands. These are very effective but be sure to read the mixing instructions and follow them accurately.

Remember that your baby will not dehydrate unless the amount of fluid lost through vomiting and/or diarrhoea is more than you are able to get back into your baby. So he will not dehydrate after one or two vomits or one or two diarrhoea stools. The trick is to give the solution frequently in small volumes even while the baby is in the vomiting phase. Aim to give about 25 ml of solution at a time and repeat this every 15 – 20 minutes. Continue to give the solution at this rate as long as your baby wants to drink and is not vomiting. If he refuses the solution, try giving it in 5 ml amounts on a teaspoon. There are some babies who refuse to drink the solution and in this situation give whatever fluid they will not vomit, including milk.

There is no reason to stop your baby's milk feeds if he has gastroenteritis. The milk products only become a problem if he develops chronic diarrhoea (that is after ten days of diarrhoea). The same goes for food. If your toddler wants to eat food, offer the food as long as he does not vomit. If you are at the point where no matter what you give, your baby vomits, you must seek medical help.

Please note that commercial energy drinks or flat Coke is not as good as ORS and should preferably not be used to rehydrate a baby.

> **SENSE-ABLE FEEDING**
> Make your own oral rehydration solution by adding 1 level teaspoon of salt and 8 level teaspoons of sugar to 1 litre of boiled water that has been cooled down. Stir thoroughly to dissolve.

When to call the doctor

The **danger** signs in this illness are:
- Persistent high fever that does not settle easily.
- Dehydration – if more fluids are going out than going in, the tongue and inside of his mouth is dry, eyes glazed and sunken, the baby passing less urine than normal, is more lethargic and tired than normal.
- Blood in the stools.
- Gastro in babies under three months.

PREVENTING ILLNESS

There is no medical intervention or treatment that has saved as many lives or prevented as much suffering as vaccination. Vaccinating your baby will help to keep him healthy by preventing some of the most serious illnesses that can affect children.

All vaccines activate the immune system to develop a memory for the infecting organism that causes the disease. The immune system is therefore primed, or on high alert, and if the real organism gets into the body, the immune system is able to wipe it out.

The vaccination schedule

The vaccination schedule tells us when the basic vaccines should be given. The South African schedule is as follows:

Age	Vaccine	How and where given
At birth	BCG (*Bacilles Calmette Guerin against TB*) OPV (0) *Oral Polio* Vaccine	Vaccination right arm Drops by mouth
6 weeks	OPV (1) *Oral Polio* Vaccine RV (1) *Rotavirus* Vaccine DTaP-IPV//Hib (1) *Diphtheria, Tetanus, acellular Pertussis, Inactivated Polio Vaccine and Haemophilius influenza type B* combined *Hepatitis B* (1) Vaccine PVC7 (1) *Pneumococcal* Conjugated Vaccine	Drops by mouth Liquid by mouth Intramuscular injection left thigh Intramuscular injection right thigh Intramuscular injection right thigh
10 weeks	DTaP-IPV//Hib (2) *Diphtheria, Tetanus, acellular Pertussis, Inactivated Polio Vaccine and Haemophilius influenza type B* combined *Hepatitis B* (2) Vaccine	Intramuscular injection left thigh Intramuscular injection right thigh
14 weeks	RV (2) *Rotavirus* Vaccine DTaP-IPV//Hib (3) *Diphtheria, Tetanus, acellular Pertussis, Inactivated Polio Vaccine and Haemophilius influenza type B* combined *Hepatitis B* (3) Vaccine PVC7 (2) *Pneumococcal* Conjugated Vaccine	Liquid by mouth Intramuscular injection left thigh Intramuscular injection right thigh Intramuscular injection right thigh
9 months	*Measles* Vaccine (1) PVC7 (3) *Pneumococcal* Conjugated Vaccine	Intramuscular injection left thigh Intramuscular injection right thigh
18 months	DTaP-IPV//Hib (4) *Diphtheria, Tetanus, acellular Pertussis, Inactivated Polio Vaccine and Haemophilius influenza type B* combined Measles Vaccine (2)	Intramuscular injection left arm Intramuscular injection right arm
6 years	Td Vaccine *Tetanus* and reduced strength of *Diphtheria* Vaccine	Intramuscular injection left arm
12 years	Td Vaccine *Tetanus* and reduced strength of *Diphtheria* Vaccine	Intramuscular injection left arm

Used with kind permission of the Department of Health

FREE VACCINES

The free vaccines supplied by the government are just as effective and safe as any vaccines available from private clinics or pharmacy clinics.

Your private clinic in South Africa can offer you a few vaccines that are not included in the government schedule, namely against Measles, Mumps and German Measles or Rubella (MMR), Varilrix against Chickenpox, and vaccines against Hepatitis A and the Human Papilloma Virus. The 6 in 1 vaccine, Infanrix Hexa, offers protection against Diphtheria, Tetanus and acellular Pertussis (whooping cough), Hymophylus influenzae type B, Polio and Hepatitis B.

Side effects and complications

Pain at the injection site with swelling is the most common side effect of vaccinations. Five per cent of children have bouts of crying, fever and irritability for up to 48 hours after the injection and this occurs most often with the DPT vaccine. The resulting introduction of acellular pertussis (aP) vaccine decreases the risk of side effects by about half.

Live virus vaccines have the potential to cause a mild form of the disease they are to prevent. This is most prevalent with the vaccine for measles, with a slight rash and fever occurring ten to fourteen days after the vaccine is administered.

There are very few reasons why vaccines should be delayed. If your baby is sick with a high fever, delay the vaccine until he is well. The following are **not** reasons to delay vaccines:

- Minor illness with fever lower than 38.5°C
- Diarrhoea
- Respiratory infections/Common cold
- Prematurity
- Family history of convulsions
- Cerebral palsy, Down's syndrome
- Chronic illness of heart, kidney, liver
- Allergies/asthma, eczema

IMMUNE SYSTEM BOOSTERS

Even healthy babies and toddlers who attend crèche are likely to get at least eight infections per year. These are generally infections of the upper respiratory tract such as a common cold or sinusitis. The infections don't occur because your baby has a weakened immune system, but because he is being exposed to bacteria and viruses that are new to the immune system. Giving him immune system boosters will not provide added protection.

Every time the immune system is exposed to a virus that it has not previously seen, it is supposed to fight off this virus. To fight off the virus the immune system will generate a fever and will produce mucus in the airway. The illness usually lasts seven to ten days and then your baby recovers. The next time he is exposed to the same virus the illness is much less severe. This is why children tend to get better and have far fewer infections after the age of four. By this time they have been exposed to the vast majority of normally occurring viruses and the immune system has memory for these viruses.

Trust your baby's wonderful built-in immunity to develop and if he does fall ill, keep a level head and keep him comfortable. Remember that illness will impact on his eating but he will most likely bounce back faster than you would imagine.

CHAPTER 8

Simple feeding sense for pregnancy

Your diet and what you consume during pregnancy has a direct bearing on your baby's development both in the womb and throughout her life. While it is not a good idea to eat for two, you will do well to eat with two in mind. Your developing baby receives her nutrition to grow and develop directly from the placenta, through your blood supply. Whatever gets into your blood stream can potentially cross the placenta and get into your baby's blood stream. This includes not only beneficial proteins, sugars, fats, vitamins, electrolytes and minerals, but also any medication and toxic substances like alcohol, nicotine and habit-forming drugs. For this reason your diet during pregnancy and what you ingest – healthy or toxic – warrant a separate chapter in this book.

WHAT TO EXPECT IN TERMS OF EATING

- You will find that many of your waking thoughts will centre on your health, how you feel and the safety of your baby.
- You may go through patches of feeling nauseous and may even vomit – this is usually in the first trimester.
- Heartburn may raise its ugly head in the last trimester as your uterus pushes on your digestive system.
- You will gain weight (between 5 and 18 kg) during the nine-month period.
- Your appetite will increase in the first two trimesters but towards the end of pregnancy will decrease as your tummy is squashed by the growing baby so there is less room for food.
- You will need a prenatal supplement to ensure your baby is getting all the nutrients she needs.
- You will feel tired and need rest, and a diet that provides you with sustainable energy.

WHAT YOUR BABY IS UP TO
The first trimester

During the first trimester of your pregnancy your baby's little body develops almost completely – not only her limbs and fingers, but also her brain and every other organ. The brain cells grow and move to their correct place in the brain, for instance a brain cell for seeing to the sight area and one for speech to the speech centre. We call this migration and it forms the basis of your baby's intelligence and who she will be. This migration is very strongly influenced by the substances you ingest during the first trimester. Drugs and alcohol in particular have a harmful effect on this process.

By 12 weeks gestation your baby looks like a miniature version of what she will be at birth. From here on she will only really grow in size and her brain, organs and lungs will mature. It is therefore crucial that you eat a healthy diet from the very beginning to give your baby the best start in life.

Second trimester

During the second trimester most of your baby's internal organs develop further and are starting to grow to the size that they need to be to help your baby live outside of your womb. Your baby needs specific nutritional elements to grow and develop properly, for example plenty of calcium for bone development. You will both need iron. Obviously, you will both benefit if you stick to a healthy and nutritious meal plan during the second trimester, too.

The third trimester

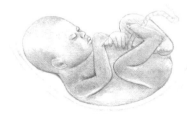

The third trimester is dedicated to the intensive growth of your baby. She will gain half her birth weight during this period. In the final months there will be further essential lung and brain development. At this stage essential fats, Omega 3 and 6, are critical for your baby's growing brain. The food you eat during the final three months is directly utilized in increasing your baby's birth weight. The quality of the food you eat continues to be of primary importance.

FEEDING YOURSELF AND YOUR BABY
Before conception

If you are in the position to plan your pregnancy, your diet is a sure way to give your baby a great start. Both you and even your partner should be eating a healthy diet. Research indicates that sperm from a healthy man in good shape on a healthy diet with limited alcohol will improve the health of a baby resulting from fertilization.

Eliminate junk food, processed foods, trans fats (processed fats) and excess sugar from your diet. Focus on eating lean protein, fruits and vegetables, whole grains, dairy and healthy fats like olive oil and avocados. These foods will also form the basis of your diet once you are pregnant, so it's a good habit to get into.

It is wise to start taking a folic acid supplement (800-1 000µg daily) if you are trying to conceive. This will reduce the risk of birth defects.

First trimester

Nausea may reduce your appetite, you may have certain cravings and be tired all the time. Your diet can have a bearing on these symptoms.

WEIGHT GAIN IN FIRST TRIMESTER

It is generally in the third month of pregnancy that you will begin to gain weight and your waistline begins to disappear. It is advisable to gain 1-2 kg in the first trimester. Of course, this will vary from woman to woman. If you are already gaining significant weight (more than 3 kg) you may be eating too much. Remember to eat healthily, not for two!

NAUSEA AND MORNING SICKNESS

Many women suffer from morning sickness in the first trimester, which can make it difficult to follow a healthy diet. It tends to be more severe in the first pregnancy or if you're carrying more than one baby. Morning sickness is a misnomer, since it can strike at any time of the day or night. Most women who experience nausea notice a dramatic improvement after the first trimester – at roughly 13 weeks. But for some the nausea and vomiting continue beyond the first trimester.

Everyone responds to food differently – most women can tolerate light and relatively bland foods, like yogurt, cereal and fruit. Fruit smoothies are a popular choice with women suffering from morning sickness. Some find that spicy foods actually help them feel better. Listen to your own body to determine what's right for you. Follow these simple steps to relieve nausea and vomiting:

- Choose small, light meals or snacks at frequent intervals.
- Before getting out of bed in the morning, eat a couple of cream crackers or a piece of dry toast.
- Have a small snack at bedtime or when you wake up to go to the bathroom in the middle of the night.
- Avoid greasy, rich, fatty and spicy foods.
- Suck on hard sweets.
- Because you lose fluids when vomiting, it is important to take in enough liquids. Try sucking on ice chips or ice lollies. Take frequent small sips of water instead of drinking a whole glass of water all at once. Some women find that taking small sips of ginger ale or peppermint tea relieves their symptoms.

Throwing up several times a day may make it difficult for you to retain adequate fluids, which is a health concern for you and your baby. Call your doctor if:

- You have not been able to keep liquids down for more than one day.
- You're vomiting blood, which may appear bright red or look like black coffee granules.
- You lose more than 1 kg.
- You have vomited more than four times in one day.

SENSE-ABLE FEEDING
Check with your doctor before using any natural remedies alleged to relieve nausea and vomiting during pregnancy.

CONSTIPATION

Hormones are responsible for early pregnancy constipation. If you are uncomfortable, consult your healthcare provider as you need to prevent piles. Eating a well-balanced diet with lots of fruit and vegetables and drinking sufficient water will assist as well. (See tips left.)

Second trimester

Healthy eating and nutrition during the second trimester of pregnancy are just as important, if not even more important, than during the first and the third trimesters of pregnancy. It is at this stage that you are providing your baby's developing organs and systems with the nutrients necessary for growth. In addition, nutritious foods, specifically proteins and iron, contribute to the health of your placenta.

WEIGHT GAIN IN SECOND TRIMESTER

Your normal clothes will become tight and uncomfortable, and you will want to start wearing soft or loose-fitting clothing. During the sixth month of pregnancy you will gain a lot of weight. By the end of the second trimester you will have gained a total of between 4 and 12 kg. (See page 96 for healthy weight gain according to your pre-pregnancy weight.)

CONSTIPATION

In your second trimester you will experience a boost in energy levels. You will feel healthier and be able to exercise more, which will help prevent constipation. In addition, as your nausea abates, you will be able to eat a greater variety of fresh fruit and vegetables, and fibre-rich foods, which will also alleviate constipation. If your constipation persists, discuss your prenatal vitamin supplement with your doctor as some supplements contain high doses of iron that may aggravate constipation.

Third trimester

Your appetite will diminish towards the end of the third trimester as there is simply less space for food in your stomach. Your energy levels will decrease and in general you slow down in preparation for the birth.

WEIGHT GAIN IN THIRD TRIMESTER

You continue to gain about 500 g per week during the seventh and eighth months. Your weight may stabilize and you may even drop a kilogram during the ninth month.

CONSTIPATION

Your first trimester niggle with constipation will return owing to lack of space in your ever accommodating abdomen. The hormone relaxin is released to loosen your ligaments in preparation for birth and you will find that your bowel is relaxed in the process. As your bowel relaxes, it slows down the movement of food and more water is absorbed from the food, which increases the risk of constipation. Keep following a balanced diet, drink sufficient fluids and remain active.

Staying on top of health and nutrition during pregnancy means avoiding certain foods:
- Raw meats and seafood, including sushi.
- Refrigerated smoked seafood such as smoked salmon.
- Raw eggs which are present in eggnog, some deserts and homemade marshmallows and mayonnaise.
- Fish high in mercury such as swordfish, king mackerel and tilefish.
- Soft cheese is only safe to eat if it is labelled pasteurized. Be cautious with Feta, Brie and Camembert cheeses, blue-veined cheeses, Queso Blanco, Queso Fresco and Queso Panela.
- Refrigerated pâtés or meat spreads have the risk of listeria contamination. It is safe to eat the canned or shelf-stable versions.
- Liver is a rich source of iron. However, it has a high vitamin A content. Large amounts of vitamin A can be harmful to your baby.
- Unpasteurised milk and juices.
- Alcohol.

SENSE-ABLE FEEDING
Alcohol use during pregnancy causes many documented foetal abnormalities and has been associated with birth defects.

NUTRITIONAL NEEDS IN PREGNANCY

There's no magic formula for a healthy pregnancy diet. As you will see from the meal plan, the basic principles of healthy eating remain the same – plenty of fruits, vegetables, whole grains and lean protein. However, some nutrients in a pregnancy diet deserve special attention. Here's what tops the list.

Protein to promote growth

Protein is crucial for your baby's growth, especially during the second and third trimesters. You should include a portion of protein (a fist size) with each meal and snack to ensure an adequate protein intake.

Good sources: Lean meat, poultry, fish and eggs are great sources of protein. Other options include dried beans and peas, tofu, dairy products and peanut butter.

Folate and folic acid to prevent birth defects

Folate is a B vitamin that helps prevent serious abnormalities of the brain and spinal cord, such as *Spina bifida*. Lack of folate in a pregnancy diet may also increase the risk of preterm delivery. The synthetic form of folate in supplements and fortified foods is known as folic acid. You need 800-1 000 µg of folic acid per day before conception and during pregnancy.

Good sources: Fortified cereals are great sources of folic acid. Leafy green vegetables, citrus fruits, and dried beans and peas are good sources of folate.

Calcium to strengthen bones

You and your baby need calcium for strong bones and teeth. Calcium also helps your circulatory, muscular and nervous systems run normally. If there's not enough calcium in your pregnancy diet, the calcium your baby needs will be taken from your bones. You need 1 000 mg a day. Pregnant teenagers need 1 300 mg a day.

Good sources: Dairy products are the richest sources of calcium. Many fruit juices and breakfast cereals are fortified with calcium.

Iron to prevent anaemia

Your body uses iron to make haemoglobin, part of the red blood cells that carries oxygen to your tissues. During pregnancy your blood volume expands to accommodate changes in your body and help your baby make her entire blood supply. As a result, your iron requirement nearly doubles to 27 mg per day. If you don't get enough iron, you may become fatigued and more susceptible to infections. The risk of preterm delivery and low birth weight may also increase.

Good sources: Lean red meat, poultry, eggs and fish are good sources of iron. Other options include iron-fortified breakfast cereals, nuts and dried fruit.

Omega 3 for the brain and eyes

The Omega 3 fatty acid, DHA, is found in high concentrations in the brain, eyes and central nervous system. Links have been made between a pregnant woman's diet rich in fish to smarter babies in the early months of life. It is important to eat foods high in Omega 3 specifically during the second and third trimesters of pregnancy, which is a time of important brain development.

Good sources: Foods high in these essential fats include fatty fish like salmon, tuna and pilchards. Nuts and seeds like flaxseed oil are also high in these special fats.

Fluids

Liquid intake is very important. Avoid gassy or caffeine-filled cold drinks. Rather drink six glasses of water every day and have fruit juices, preferably freshly squeezed, Rooibos tea and milk to supplement your fluid intake.

A HEALTHY MEAL PLAN FOR PREGNANCY

To eat a balanced diet during your pregnancy you should have three to five servings of fresh fruits and vegetables each day. One of these should be a dark orange vegetable, and two should be leafy, dark green vegetables. You should have three to six servings of extra-lean meats, chicken, fish, or cooked peas or dried beans, six servings of grains and starches, and three servings of fat free or low fat milk products.

	Monday	Tuesday	Wednesday	Thursday	Friday	Saturday	Sunday
Breakfast	1 cup high-fibre cereal with 1 cup low-fat milk, berry smoothie	1 boiled egg, 1 slice whole-wheat toast, medium apple	1 cup high-fibre cereal with 1 cup low-fat milk, ½ pawpaw	1 boiled egg, 1 slice whole-wheat toast, berry smoothie	1 cup high-fibre cereal with 1 cup low-fat milk, ½ pawpaw	1 slice whole-wheat toast with processed cheese, berry smoothie	1 cup high-fibre cereal with 1 cup low-fat milk, ½ pawpaw
Snack	1 apple, 100 g low-fat yoghurt	1 muffin	2 Provitas with cottage cheese, ham & tomato	100 g low-fat yoghurt, grapes	1 muffin	2 Provitas with cottage cheese, ham & tomato	1 wholewheat scone and grated cheese
Lunch	Salmon on whole wheat bread with salad	1 matchbox size block of cheese whole-wheat sand-wich, salad, 1 naartjie or grapefruit	1 portion cooked chicken, ½ cup raw or cooked vegetable (beans, broc-coli, etc.)	Tuna salad with tomato, cucumber & feta cheese, 1 slice whole-wheat bread	1 bowl vegeta-ble soup with wholegrain roll, medium apple, ¾ cup fruit juice	1 portion salmon on whole-wheat roll with salad	Beef wrap with salad and fruit
Snack	2 Provitas with cottage cheese, ham & tomato	100 g low-fat yogurt, grapes	100 g low-fat yogurt, medium apple	2 Provitas with cottage cheese, ham & tomato	100 g low fat yogurt, medium apple	2 Provitas with cream cheese, ham & tomato	An afternoon treat e.g. a piece of chocolate cake and Rooibos latte
Dinner	Chicken à la King with ½ cup brown rice, peas & onion	57 g meat, potatoes (done the way you prefer), salad	Hake fillet portion, baby potatoes, salad	Pasta with vegetable sauce, fruit salad	1 portion chicken, por-tion potatoes, spinach, rosa tomatoes	1 grilled salmon fillet, salad with avocado, to-mato, cheese & lemon juice	Bowl of butternut soup, 1 slice seed loaf and avocado topping
Bedtime snack	1 glass low-fat/skim milk, 1 wholewheat biscuit	1 glass low-fat/skim milk, 1 wholewheat biscuit	1 glass low-fat/skim milk, 1 wholewheat biscuit	1 glass low-fat/skim milk, 1 wholewheat biscuit	1 glass low-fat/skim milk, 1 wholewheat biscuit	1 glass low-fat/skim milk, 1 wholewheat biscuit	1 glass low-fat/skim milk, 1 wholewheat biscuit

HEALTHY WEIGHT GAIN – HAVE YOU HAD ENOUGH?

There's no one-size-fits-all approach to pregnancy weight gain. How much weight you need to gain depends on various factors, including your pre-pregnancy weight and body mass index (BMI). Your health and your baby's health also play a role. Work with your healthcare provider to determine what's right for you. Consider these general guidelines for pregnancy weight gain:

Pre-pregnancy weight	Recommended weight gain
Underweight (BMI less than 18.5)	13-18 kg
Normal weight (BMI 18.5 to 24.9)	11-16 kg
Overweight (BMI 25 to 29.9)	7-11 kg
Obese (BMI 30 or greater)	5-9 kg

If you're carrying twins or multiples, you will likely need to gain more weight. Again, work with your healthcare provider to determine what's right for you.

Although excess weight carries risks – such as gestational diabetes and high blood pressure – pregnancy isn't the time to lose weight. Even if you're overweight before pregnancy, it's important to gain a healthy amount of weight during pregnancy. Do keep an eye on the scale, though. If you gain more than the recommended amount during pregnancy and you don't lose the weight after your baby is born, the excess kilograms carry life-long health risks. It's more important to avoid overeating and make healthy choices. Consider these suggestions:

* Trade white bread and pasta for the wholegrain variety.
* Choose a salad with low-fat dressing and chicken breast instead of a fast food take-away.
* Eat sliced fruit instead of a biscuit.

YOUR BABY'S HEALTH
Supplements

The amount of nutrients available to your baby is entirely dependent on your nutritional status. If you are eating a well-balanced diet of fresh food, your baby will receive most of the nutrients she needs. This is the reason why it is so important for you to maintain a good and healthy lifestyle during pregnancy. However, even with the best diet, there are certain key micronutrients that you will need to supplement. A good prenatal vitamin will contain:

* Calcium 1 000 mg
* Folic Acid 800 ug
* Iron 27 mg
* Vitamin A not more than 5000 iu
* Varying amounts of vitamin B, C and other minerals
* If it does not contain Omega 3 and you are not eating enough fatty fish and nuts, add an Omega 3 supplement.

Most of the transfer of vitamins and minerals occurs in the last trimester (after 28 weeks of pregnancy). Premature babies therefore lose out on this and require additional vitamins and minerals shortly after birth. This is standard care and vitamins and minerals are given to premature babies from 7-10 days of life.

Alcohol and drugs

Alcohol abuse during pregnancy will affect your baby and cause Foetal Alcohol Syndrome (FAS) – a condition that causes developmental delay, learning difficulties and specific features in the face: small head, flat and long upper lip with a thin lip line and short stature. Current thinking is that not only regular consumption of substantial quantities of alcohol, but also drinking binges will lead to FAS. In some cases as little as one binge may be sufficient to cause signs of FAS. In addition, Foetal Alcohol Effects (FAE), which include learning disabilities and ADD, may result from random social drinking in pregnancy. The amount of alcohol that can cause these problems is not known, and this is one of the situations where complete avoidance is best. **Don't drink alcohol during pregnancy.**

Smoking during pregnancy is extremely dangerous for your baby because it causes:
- Growth restriction in your baby, resulting in small and low-weight babies
- Decreased breast-milk production
- Increased risk of asthma and lung disease.

Drug addiction and the recreational use of drugs cause serious problems in your foetus, ranging from deformities and mental retardation to premature birth and withdrawal symptoms. The withdrawal symptoms are difficult to treat and extremely dangerous for the newborn.

Medication

The use of medication during pregnancy is often unavoidable and you therefore need to think clearly about it to make informed decisions. All registered medications must indicate whether they are safe in pregnancy and breast-feeding or not. The extent of any risk is known for most medications. If this has not been accurately determined, the information on the medication will state that safety has not been established. If you have to take medication, check with your pharmacist and/or doctor.

It is essential that you remain in good health during your pregnancy. If this requires chronic medication, e.g. for diabetes, epilepsy, hypertension, asthma or depression, it is essential that you continue with the safest medication available. If you fall ill, e.g. pneumonia, bladder infection, migraines or any other condition, it is important to get better as fast as possible and taking medication will allow this. Once again, check with you doctor.

Allergy prevention

There is a lot of research on this topic. While you may be advised to avoid foods that you think may cause allergy in your baby, we now know that this is not true.

You will not prevent allergies in your baby by avoiding allergenic foods such as fish and peanuts. If you are allergic to certain foods you must obviously avoid them in pregnancy.

COMMON ISSUES FOR PREGNANCY
Food cravings – PICA

Almost every TV comedy featuring a pregnant woman will show her eating something strange like pickles with ice cream. While eating strange combinations of food or eating a lot of a certain type of food is common, pica is something altogether different. Pica is a condition of craving substances with little or no nutritional value. Most pica cravings involve non-food substances such as dirt or chalk. *Pica* is the Latin word for *magpie*, a bird notorious for eating almost anything.

The most common substances craved during pregnancy are dirt, clay, and laundry starch. Other pica cravings include: burnt matches, stones, charcoal, mothballs, ice, cornstarch, toothpaste, soap, sand, plaster, coffee grounds, baking soda, and cigarette ashes.

If you find yourself craving weird foods or non-food substances, don't panic; it happens and is not abnormal. The most important thing is to inform your healthcare provider to make sure you have a complete understanding of the specific risks associated with your cravings. Here are some suggestions to help you deal with pica cravings:

- Inform your healthcare provider and review your prenatal health records
- Monitor your iron status along with your general vitamin and mineral intake
- Consider potential substitutes for the cravings such as chewing sugarless gum
- Inform a friend of your craving, who can help you avoid non-food items.

Heartburn

You may find that the pressure from your growing foetus puts pressure on your digestive tract, forcing stomach contents back up through the oesophagus. You can minimize acid reflux or heartburn by eating small, regular meals, chewing food thoroughly, and eating slowly. Don't lie down for at least an hour after eating. Certain foods may cause worse symptoms of heartburn than others, and should be avoided or restricted:

- Too many refined starches like cakes and white bread
- Spicy foods like curries and chilli sauces
- Rich, creamy foods like cream sauces and gravies
- Overeating at any meal, no matter what the food is, will also make the symptoms of heartburn worse.

Your diet in pregnancy is a gift you give your baby. By watching what you eat you will provide her with the best start in life. In addition, you will prepare yourself for birth, breast-feeding and for those early days of parenthood when you are tired and the demands on your body are significant.

CHAPTER 9

Simple feeding sense for your prem baby

In all likelihood during pregnancy, you envisaged your first feed to be within hours of your little one's birth, guided by supportive nursery staff who would help your baby to latch. You probably eagerly anticipated the closeness of that first breast-feed. Faced with the premature birth of your baby, your experience has probably been anything but this. Not only have you lost the dream you had of the perfect birth, but you also have to cope with losing all the normal experiences of a new mom – holding and feeding your newborn. You may be weeks away from holding and feeding him or it may only be a matter of days. Either way, this chapter will prepare you for the stages of feeding a prem baby.

WHAT TO EXPECT IN TERMS OF FEEDING AT THIS STAGE

- If your prem baby is born very early or is sick, he will be fed through tubes and/ or even drips in the early days.
- It will take time for the sucking reflex to become established and you need to encourage non-nutritive sucking.
- From 28 weeks gestation, you can expect your healthy prem baby to start developing the sucking reflex. But many premature babies only begin to coordinate suck, swallow and breathing after 32 weeks.
- Once your baby can coordinate suck, swallow and breathing, and can maintain an awake state, he will be ready for breast or bottle feeds.

WHAT YOUR BABY IS UP TO
Development

Not having the benefit of being curled up in the last few weeks *in utero*, your prem baby will have lower **muscle tone** than a full-term baby. He will be carefully positioned in the incubator to enhance his muscle tone. This is important because as he grows, he will need good muscle tone to suck effectively, to hold his head up for solids and later to chew his food. Good positions in the incubator are best obtained with a specially designed nest or rolled blanket that is:

- Made of 100% cotton for temperature regulation
- A soft but firm boundary that touches your prem baby's head and feet
- Washable.

The very best environment for your prem baby to grow and thrive is on your body. Your skin is your little prem baby's natural environment, and as soon as he is ready, you will be encouraged to hold him skin to skin, also known as Kangaroo Care. This skin to skin contact is used extensively in neonatal units throughout the world. Place your prem baby with only a nappy and a hat on, naked on your naked chest and turn his head to one side so that his ear is against your chest between your breasts. Cover him with a blanket or wear a Kangaroo Care top. Your chest temperature will increase a degree or two to warm up your baby and will maintain a constant temperature for him. Do this *as much as possible* with your prem baby as soon as the NICU staff give the go ahead – usually when he is relatively stable. Research indicates that Kangaroo Care can enhance parent-child bonding, promote breast-feeding, and improve a preemie's health.

The optimal position for your baby to grow, develop and stay calm is **curled** towards his belly button, with a straight neck. He may be positioned on his **side** so that his arms are brought together and close to his face, which makes him feel more contained. If your baby is lying on his **back**, support his head on a gel or memory foam mattress or pillow to prevent flattening of his head; his head should be in line with his spine. Use a boundary or nest to support his legs and shoulders so that he is slightly curled up and not flat on his back in a froglike position. At times, your prem baby will be on his **tummy**. This is a nice position for breathing, absorption of feeds and development, and will make him feel secure. Since his breathing is monitored, there is no risk of SIDS (cot death) in this position.

If your baby was born before 36 weeks gestation, there is a good chance his **primitive reflexes** are not developed yet. The primitive reflexes pertaining to feeding that need time to develop, are the rooting (turning towards touch on his cheek – this helps him find a source of food, such as your nipple) and sucking reflexes (sucking motions with the tongue the second something touches his tongue and the roof of his mouth). The sucking reflex in particular is a critical reflex for feeding and you will need to assist your prem to develop this reflex. Until he does, you will not be able to breast or bottle feed him. The best way to develop this reflex and to strengthen it is to give your baby the opportunity to suck on a clean finger or a specially sized prem dummy. You can give one to your baby after every feed and during any tube feeds.

Sensory

Your new prem will be **very sensitive** and the stimulation that comes with just being alive is as much as he will manage. It may be some time before he can cope with the sensory demands of being held for a feed, and interacting with you will take time and generally emerges in three phases:

PAUSE PHASE

If your baby was born very premature – before 32 weeks – his interactions will be characterized by the word *pause*: he will pause rather than engage and you should pause before interacting with him. In this phase your baby may be too medically fragile to feed. Even the simplest sensory interaction of light touch can cause him to become disorganized and stressed. He is focusing all his energy on just maintaining stable vital signs and growing. Your baby may well be fed by drip or tube during this phase. Some babies are able to suck well enough to cope with breast-feeding although they are the exception.

TOUCH PHASE

As your little one gets older (between 32 and 35 weeks) he will start to emerge from the pause phase into the *touch* phase. He will be medically stable, will cope with your touch and may even learn a few self-soothing strategies. He is no longer acutely ill and begins to gain weight as he absorbs calories from his feeds. During this stage your baby will develop his sucking reflex and will soon manage to suck from your breast or a teat.

ENGAGE PHASE

From 36 weeks onwards your baby begins to interact actively with his world and invites you to engage with him. He is much like a full-term newborn and can cope with more interaction, but does tend to become overstimulated when faced with too much sensory input at once. You will be giving your baby every feed at this stage.

FEEDING YOUR PREM BABY

Feeding can be a very stressful process for parents of premature babies and is often a huge source of anxiety and concern. It is important to remember that your baby will develop at his own pace and should always be cared for as an individual. Although the milk you produce is perfectly designed for a new-born baby, the needs of premature babies can be complicated. Your breast milk may be supplemented with extra nutrients using a special powder that contains additional protein and energy (FM85).

Immediately after birth, the goal is to stabilize your baby's medical condition. Once this has been accomplished, the paediatrician and the NICU (neonatal intensive care unit) staff will discuss feeding options with you to maximise growth and development of his tiny body.

> **SENSE-ABLE FEEDING**
> Your premature baby may not be able to be fed by mouth in the beginning, or may not be strong enough to take in *enough* milk to grow.

Early forms of feeding

It is essential that premature babies are started on feeds within the first 24-48 hours of life. Very small, very sick and very premature babies are initially fed via a 'drip' into their vein or belly button. This type of feed is known as **Total Parenteral Nutrition** (TPN) and contains nutrients such as glucose, protein and fats. TPN is used when a baby's digestive system is immature, as too much energy would be used for digestion if he was fed by mouth. By passing the nutrients directly into his bloodstream, TPN enables your baby to feed without using his energy to eat and absorb the nutrients required to grow and thrive.

To begin with, TPN may be the only source of nutrition for very prem or sick babies. But as your baby grows and becomes stronger, a method called **tube feeding** will be introduced, usually within the first two days, and slowly increased to avoid overloading the absorption capacity of the stomach and intestines. With this feed nutrients pass directly into your baby's stomach through a fine tube placed in the mouth or the nose. Once tube feeding has been successfully set up, TPN will stop.

Tube feeding ensures that your baby receives enough nutrients from breast milk or formula to grow and thrive. Most premature and sick babies will be fed in this way as they are too small or sick to suck to feed. Sucking at a breast or bottle takes energy and coordination and it may be a few weeks before your baby is ready for this.

You may notice your baby opening and closing his mouth, moving his tongue or sucking his fingers during a tube feed. This shows he is ready to practise sucking. It is a good idea when you see this to offer him a prem dummy or your clean finger to suck on – this non-nutritive sucking will help strengthen his suck reflex in preparation to feed without a tube.

Unlike the medical procedures in the Neonatal Intensive Care Unit (NICU), feeding is often something in which you can participate. No matter which method is used to feed your baby, there is probably a way you can be involved. Many NICUs will encourage parents in this manner since it promotes bonding and indeed your baby's health.

Breast-feeding your prem baby

Not only does breast-feeding a premature baby offer all the benefits a term baby receives, but a premature baby also derives several preemie-specific benefits from breast milk:

- It provides antibodies that protect your prem baby against bacteria and viruses. Premature breast milk is extra rich in antibodies and growth factors.
- It boosts your baby's immune system and protects against infections, such as ear, stomach and chest infections.
- It provides nutrients and growth hormones that help your baby grow and develop during the vital early months after birth.
- It is very easy to digest and is absorbed more easily than formula milk.
- It allows you to have skin to skin contact with your baby. Research has shown that this is very beneficial, especially for premature babies.

EXPRESSING BREAST MILK

To stimulate your milk supply, you should express as soon as possible after birth (preferably within four hours). Initially you will only express colostrum, which is highly nutritious and will be given to your baby. When your milk comes in, breast milk can be frozen and stored until your baby is ready to feed or given to your baby via tube feeds.

If your prem baby is too weak to suck, especially if he was born before 34 weeks, breast milk must be expressed and given via a feeding tube. If you'd like to give your baby breast milk but don't know where to start, talk to your doctor or someone on the hospital staff. Most places equipped to care for preemies also have professionals available to help you with the ins and outs of pumping, storing, and feeding breast milk to premature infants.

MOVING ON TO BREAST-FEEDING

Once your baby is strong enough to feed at the breast, you might have to experiment to find a position that is comfortable, and also gives your baby extra head support to facilitate sucking. A lactation consultant can be very helpful as you make this transition.

If your baby is able to suck only a small amount at a time, you might want to express breast milk as well as breast-feed in order to establish a good milk supply. It's best to pump milk from the breast from which your baby nursed only a little or not at all. Then at the next feed, offer this breast first.

If your baby is well enough to come out of the incubator, give him lots of opportunities to be at your breast so he can enjoy being close and, when he is more mature and interested enough, he will start licking milk and, eventually, practice-sucking. It's a good idea to have him at the breast while he is having a tube-feed.

Premature babies won't breast-feed 'properly' and take much milk until they are mature enough to coordinate breathing, sucking and swallowing. But although sucking practice does not provide them with a feed, it's important for their digestion, growth and well-being, and boosts your milk supply.

Bottle feeds

Bottle feeding a preemie is very different from feeding a full-term infant. Using a special prem teat and bottle, your options for bottle feeding your baby are:

- To express breast milk and feed your baby your own breast milk (this is preferable because your milk is well suited to your baby and has a protective effect on the digestive tract).
- To feed your baby breast milk from a breast milk bank or another mother – this provides the same benefits to the intestines.
- If there is no chance of breast milk, feed your baby a prem baby formula or a semi-elemental or amino-based formula if your prem is at risk of NEC (see page 105).

Unlike a baby born at full term, a premature baby may be very sleepy at feed times, may not be strong enough to drink enough milk to sustain growth, and may have a hard time swallowing and breathing at the same time. NICU nurses will help you learn how to bottle feed your preemie.

> **SENSE-ABLE FEEDING**
> It is important to know that now, more than at any stage in your baby's life, breast milk provides the optimal nutrition and protection for your baby.

NUTRITIONAL NEEDS OF PREM BABIES

Your prem baby needs more fluid and calories per kilogram of body weight than full-term, and small-for-dates babies as he has a lot of catching up to do. Although newborns in general grow substantially during their first 12 months, the process is especially accelerated for preemies. A prem baby's birth weight often increases by up to five times in the first year; in comparison, full-term babies usually only triple their birth weight over that same period of time.

Necessary nutrients

Your premature baby may have been born before his body had the chance to store certain important nutrients needed for growth, including iron, fat, protein, vitamins A, D, and E, calcium, phosphorous, magnesium and other trace minerals. It's essential that these nutrients be provided after birth for proper body functioning and to create some stores. Breast milk fat is well absorbed and is rich in long-chain polyunsaturated fatty acids Omega 3 and Omega 6. These are important for brain, eye and nerve development. It's particularly important for prem babies to get plenty of Omega 3 as they miss out on the large amount of Omega 3 transferred via the placenta in the last weeks of a full-term pregnancy.

A HEALTHY MEAL PLAN FOR PREM BABIES

As you approach the day your baby will be discharged you will be feeling justifiably anxious. Suddenly you and your partner are the only people responsible for this little life. While this may feel daunting, you are adequately equipped to feed your baby and ensure he thrives.

If your baby is sleepy, you may need to wake him two-hourly during the day and three-hourly at night to feed until he weighs between 3 and 4 kg.

Breast-feeding

If you are breast-feeding on discharge, you will still need to focus on establishing your milk supply. It is early days so make sure you drink lots or fluids, rest when your baby sleeps and feed on cue as your prem baby will drink small amounts frequently.

Bottle feeding

If you are bottle feeding you will be guided on how much milk your baby should be receiving and advised about ongoing supplementation and perhaps fortification as mentioned previously, before discharge. It will be helpful initially to follow a similar feeding schedule to one that was set up in hospital. You and your baby will be familiar with this routine.

Supplements

Your baby's paediatrician may recommend supplements of vitamins A, B, C, D, K, and sometimes E, as well as folic acid and iron, for up to six to 12 months. A supplement of essential fatty acids and zinc is sometimes beneficial too.

HAS MY PREM BABY HAD ENOUGH?

While your premature baby is in hospital and especially in the NICU, everything he consumes will be written down and monitored. Once he is discharged you can continue to write down his feeds so that you can track them and take the record with you for your regular clinic visits. These guidelines will also put your mind at rest:

- Most preemies need **eight to ten feeds a day** with no more than three hours between feeds. How often your baby feeds will depend strongly on his size, growth rate, age, and how early he was born. If you're not sure if he's feeding enough, or if this frequent feeding schedule seems too difficult to accomplish, talk to your healthcare professional or a lactation consultant for guidance and reassurance.
- **Six to eight wet nappies** per day show that your baby is getting enough breast milk or formula.
- Your baby will only be able to drink a **small amount** at a time, which means that he will have to be fed often. In addition, he can be easily distracted or disturbed during this process, so be sure to feed your baby in a quiet, calm place away from other children, noise, and household traffic.

Amount based on 150 ml/kg/day divided by eight feeds
For a 2,5 kg prem baby = 45 ml per feed
For a 3 kg prem baby = 55 ml per feed
For a 3,5 kg prem baby = 65 ml per feed
For a 4 kg prem baby = 75 ml per feed

YOUR BABY'S HEALTH
Infections and feeds

The most serious infection a premature baby faces is called necrotising entero-colitis (NEC). It can cause damage to the colon and intestines, lead to lifelong health complications in the prem baby and, in some cases, even result in death. This is very rare in babies who are *exclusively* breast-fed, therefore breast-feeding your premature baby is one of the most important contributions you can make to his health.

Growth

Your prem baby should catch up his growth by the end of the first year. Up to this age it is appropriate to work with his corrected rather than actual age when working out his expected weight and length. If a baby was born at 28 weeks gestation, which is 12 weeks early, then at six months of age from birth, he will only be three months old by corrected age.

> **Adjusted age calculation**
> Age – weeks premature
> = adjusted age
>
> 6 months = 24 weeks
> Born 12 weeks premature
> 24 – 12 = 12
>
> Adjusted age = 12 weeks
> 12 weeks = 3 months

Health

Follow the same vaccination schedule for your prem as for full-term babies. This means that he will get the BCG and Polio at birth and the first vaccines at six weeks of age regardless of the age of gestation. A 28-week premature baby can have the BCG and Polio at birth and the six week vaccines when he is the equivalent of 34 weeks gestation.

COMMON FEEDING ISSUES

My baby is ready to be moved from a tube feed to the next step. What comes next?

Your baby can start learning to drink by mouth if he's not on a ventilator, can coordinate breathing, swallowing and sucking, and has an efficient gag reflex. As he grows he may use several methods. For a baby on breast milk, any combination of the following:

- Cup-feed: a specially shaped prem feeding cup is a great way to feed your baby breast milk as it is easier than bottle and breast-feeding in the transition phase of feeding.
- Breast: ideally it's best to start cup and breast-feeding together.
- Breast supplementer: a thin plastic tube that runs from a receptacle over your shoulder, containing expressed breast milk to just past your nipple, delivering breast milk to your baby while he suckles at the breast.

For a formula-fed baby a cup or a special prem bottle is used.

How do I cup-feed?

You can start cup-feeding from 30-32 weeks, guided by your paediatrician. Start teaching your baby to cup-feed with the feeding tube in place, which means he may be tube- and cup-fed for several weeks.

If you're supplying breast milk:

- Shake the container of expressed breast milk and pour some into a sterilised prem baby cup. Hold your baby on your lap, preferably close to your naked breast so he smells you and your milk, and put a drop of milk on his tongue so he tastes its sweetness.
- Gently tilt the cup so it touches the lower lip and a little milk enters his mouth, but take care not to swamp him. Within a few days or weeks he'll start lapping the milk like a kitten, or sipping or sucking it. Don't worry about how much he takes; the nurses will work out whether he needs a top-up by tube.
- Make this time as peaceful and relaxed as possible, so he associates cup-feeds with pleasure and tranquillity.

During the next few weeks your baby will take increasing amounts of milk from a cup and can start feeding from the breast or bottle. He'll gradually need less and less by tube and the day will arrive when it can come out. Some mothers never cup-feed, but start teaching their babies to breast-feed with the tube in place.

Can I use another mother's breast milk that has been donated to the NICU?

If your baby is very small, if you can't provide enough milk, even with skilled help, and if he isn't doing well on formula, then it's wise to give him donated breast milk (though it's an excellent idea to continue giving as much of your own milk as you can).

Babies who particularly benefit from donated breast milk include:

- Tube-fed babies with very low birth-weight, especially in their first week, when they tolerate human milk better than formula
- Those not growing or thriving well
- Those who've had bowel surgery
- Those with a poorly functioning immune system, for example a baby who has already had an infection
- Those with diarrhoea
- Those with necrotising enterocolitis. This is six to ten times more common in formula-fed babies, but donated breast milk is as protective as a mother's own milk.

POSSIBLE FEEDING PROBLEMS RELATED TO PREMATURITY

Sensory defensiveness

During your prem baby's stay in hospital he may be exposed to painful interventions as part of his medical care. Not only is this difficult for you and your baby at the time, but in the long run these painful experiences may change your baby's response to sensory input for life. He may become very sensitive to touch and in particular touch around the mouth. It is not uncommon for prem babies to be fussy eaters later. Varied textures and specific foods may be avoided altogether. Over time, you will know the effects on your baby's sensory system and can seek the intervention of a therapist specialized in babies with feeding issues.

Reflux

Sometimes small prem babies will have digestive issues and gastroesophageal reflux. When a prem baby has trouble keeping foods down, this can prove to be a considerable problem; reflux indicates the immaturity of his digestive system. Feeding him can be improved by using medication to manage reflux issues. Keeping him in an upright position for a period of time after meals helps in diminishing the occurrence of reflux. Smaller feeds more often will give him a better chance to digest small amounts of breast milk or formula before being offered more.

Iron deficiency

Premature babies have lower iron stores at birth than term infants and therefore a higher risk of iron deficiency. Iron is needed to make red blood cells, which carry oxygen throughout the body. To improve blood iron levels your prem baby will need an iron rich supplement and once he is on solids you need to introduce him to a variety of foods containing iron.

When to start solids

Choosing the right time to introduce solid food is a challenge with any baby and the guidelines for starting preemies on solids differ greatly. Here is a guideline you can use in conjunction with advice from your clinic sister or doctor:

Fill in these dates to help you decide when to start solids	Date
Birth date	
Due date	
17 weeks after birth date	
17 weeks after due date	
Midway between the two dates is the earliest date to consider starting solids (See guidelines in Chapter 4.)	
Seven months after birth date Definitely ready to start solids by this date	
Your baby's start date	

Adapted from Auckland District Health Board: "Guidelines on starting solids for caregivers of premature babies" by Barbara Cormack

Making it through the tough early days of life with a prem baby is a big achievement. You are well equipped to cope with his feeding and other concerns regarding his health and well-being. Upon discharge you can go on to the next chapter.

Simple feeding sense from birth to six weeks

The first six weeks of motherhood are possibly the greatest learning curve of your life. You are likely to feel quite insecure at times as you realize the weight of the responsibility of caring for your little one and wonder whether you are doing the best for your baby at all times. Feeding is often the area of the most turmoil during this time as breast-feeding takes a while to establish and does not come easily for all people. In addition, you may be faced with having to decide on alternate forms of feeding if your baby is not well or not thriving. Try to find a lactation consultant to assist you if you are having a tough time.

WHAT TO EXPECT IN TERMS OF FEEDING AT THIS STAGE

- Breast-feeding takes as long as six weeks to become well established. The best way to establish your milk supply is to feed on cue.
- Wake your baby to feed if more than two to four hours have passed between feeds during the day.
- Feed your baby when she wakes at night, which may mean feeding almost as frequently at night as during the day. By six weeks, she may have one longer stretch at **night** without needing to feed.
- Most breast-fed babies will drink for 10-15 minutes on each breast or 30 minutes on one and 5 minutes on the second breast. But you shouldn't time your feeds – watch your baby rather than the clock.
- Bottle-fed babies will drink 60-90 ml every two to four hours.
- By four to eight weeks, your baby will start to get into a rhythm or pattern of feeding that is more predictable.
- If your baby is unsettled in the evening you may need to offer one or two cluster feeds – feeds close together. This may also help her to sleep for a slightly longer stretch later.
- It is important that you look after yourself properly at this stage, drinking lots of fluids and eating a nutritious diet (see page 24 for a meal plan).
- You can expect **growth spurts** (also known as frequency days) at 10-14 days and again around six weeks of age, when your baby will demand a feed more often than before.

WHAT YOUR BABY IS UP TO
Developmental

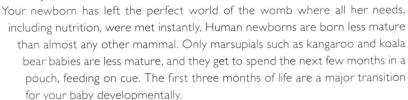

Your newborn has left the perfect world of the womb where all her needs, including nutrition, were met instantly. Human newborns are born less mature than almost any other mammal. Only marsupials such as kangaroo and koala bear babies are less mature, and they get to spend the next few months in a pouch, feeding on cue. The first three months of life are a major transition for your baby developmentally.

Your skin is your baby's natural environment and both physically and emotionally the healthiest place for her to be. Skin to skin contact in the early weeks will encourage breast-feeding, bonding and development.

Your newborn has poor head control and will need her neck to be supported. Her reflexes govern her movement and help her to feed well. Her sucking and rooting reflex guide her to your nipple and ensure she can feed. It may be some time before she can coordinate her suck, swallow and breathe well so at times your little one may choke and splutter on a milk feed, especially if the flow is fast.

Sleep

Your baby will need to **sleep** after only being awake for 45-60 minutes at a stretch. Use this awake time to feed her and for care-giving and appropriate stimulation. She should be sleeping for about 18 to 20 hours in a 24-hour cycle. You may find your baby is still very sleepy and may have her day and night muddled up – waking more at night than during the day. To address this problem, be sure to wake your baby to feed at least four-hourly during the day and leave her to sleep at night as long as she is gaining enough weight and is feeding at least six to ten times in 24 hours. Feed her quietly in a dark room when she wakes at night.

Colic and stimulation

A developmental goal of this stage is to remain calm in the presence of stimulation. From the moment of birth your baby will be faced with sensory input from the world, as well as interoception – the internal messages from her tummy and the rest of her body. Because she is immature, all this stimulation will overwhelm her at times and you may be faced with a colicky, fractious baby. The resultant **crying** has classically been known as *colic* which means 'abdominal discomfort'. It is actually not directly due to abdominal issues, nor is it necessarily hunger. Colic is usually a result of overstimulation. It peaks at six weeks and disappears by 12 weeks. If your baby is particularly fussy, you may worry that she is not getting enough milk and be tempted to supplement or replace breast milk with formula. Instead of judging whether she is hungry based on crying, rather determine whether your baby has had enough milk (see page 113).

FEEDING YOUR NEWBORN

Immediately after birth, your baby will have a period of calm-alert attention, when she will examine your face and focus on you. During this period, place your baby on your breast – it is a good time for you both to learn the basics of latching. Hold your baby in a cradle hold and bring her towards your breast (not your breast towards her). When her mouth makes contact with your nipple, she will open her mouth. Place her mouth firmly over your nipple at that moment and ensure that she latches correctly.

The "how to" of breast-feeding is discussed at length in Chapter 2 (see pages 21-31). Return to that section to refresh your memory whenever necessary. If you are uncertain how to latch your baby or whether she is correctly latched, call a lactation consultant to help you. See Resources (page 173) for a consultant in your area.

In the first 24 hours, wake your baby every three hours for a feed or feed more often if she demands. Newborns tend to sleep a lot in the early days and may need to be woken to feed. Your baby will not get 'milk' from you during these feeds but wonderful colostrum which is full of antibodies and is a concentrated source of nutrients, so you need way less colostrum than breast milk to satisfy your baby.

Once your milk comes in

Usually around the third day, your breasts will start to feel firmer as your milk changes from colostrum to milk that looks kind of like skim milk. Sometimes, for no apparent reason, a mother's milk may take longer than a few days to come in. For example, diabetes can delay the onset of milk production. Let your doctor or lactation consultant know if your milk has not come in after three days.

You will start to feel your milk flow as your baby starts to feed – we call this the **letdown reflex**. For some women it feels like a tingle while for others it is more painful. This settles after a few days and becomes more like a tingling sensation. Letdown may also occur before you start nursing (some women experience let-own from simply seeing their baby or hearing a baby cry), or it may happen after your baby is latched and has sucked a few times (you may notice your baby starting to gulp).

During the first few days to weeks after delivery, you may feel strong cramps in your uterus as you feed. It is common to feel a sense of engorgement initially, as your breasts are filling up and becoming firm, or a sort of tingling sensation in your breasts. You may also feel or see some milk leaking from your nipples. Some women never have a feeling of letdown or engorgement, which is also fine. Even if you don't feel it, you should still see milk coming from your nipple and hear your baby swallowing.

Hormonal changes are responsible for your milk coming in and you may find yourself feeling down. This often coincides with the day your milk comes in, which can be quite trying as you not only have a new baby, you are also having to cope with a flow of milk that may seem more than your baby actually needs at this stage. To help your breasts adjust to the milk coming in, feed regularly to drain them. If you still produce more milk than your baby can drink, you may become engorged. See page 116 for advice on managing this.

Your baby will probably breast-feed about 6-10 times a day – every two to four hours during the day and three to six hourly at night. You should be feeding on cue and following your baby's cues. If she cries and only one to two hours have passed since the last feed, bear in mind that not all cries are hunger cries. You can soothe your baby in other ways such as sucking on your finger or a dummy or putting her in a sling close to your body.

Most babies lose weight during their first week and then get back up to their birth weight by the time they are two weeks old.

Bottle feeding

It is important that you offer your baby the breast in the early days unless there is a very good medical reason to move her straight onto bottles. If you want to breast-feed but feel you do not have enough milk or are having a hard time, do the following:

- Call a lactation consultant immediately. The sooner you get help to latch your baby and establish breast-feeding the more likely you are to get it right.
- For 24 hours feed your baby whenever she cries. This will help you gain confidence and will help your milk come in.
- If your baby is not demanding to be fed and is sleeping a lot, wake her regularly and offer her the breast.
- In the next 48 hours continue to feed on cue and after these three days, re-evaluate how you feel about breast-feeding – there is a good chance you will be feeling better and will be able to continue successfully.

If you have chosen to bottle feed for whatever reason, you can be confident that your baby's nutritional needs will be met. Bottle feeding is discussed at length in Chapter 3 (see page 32).

- Offer your baby the breast for at least three days to ensure she gets that precious colostrum.
- Get a bottle and teat system you feel comfortable with and ensure you use a very slow flow teat.
- Begin with a basic cow's milk formula.

Waking for night feeds

At this tender age, you must expect your baby to wake up during the night. The key is to learn when you should pick her up for a night feed and when she will simply settle back to sleep. When you hear your baby at night, listen and watch her carefully. Babies are noisy sleepers and she may just be stirring in her sleep. Do not pick her up if she is simply moaning. If your baby cries at night, she will be waking from either hunger or discomfort. Feed her quietly in a dim room, keeping her calm.

SENSE-ABLE FEEDING
If breast-feeding is your choice, the only circumstance in which your baby will definitely need to be fed formula from a bottle, syringe or cup is if you are too sick to feed your baby or to express. In general, however, there is no reason to give formula top-ups in the first three days of life.

A HEALTHY MEAL PLAN FOR YOUR NEWBORN

Your baby will get all her nutrition from breast milk or an iron-fortified infant formula until she is four to six months old. Do not supplement with water, juice or cereal at this time.

In the first few weeks, feeding on cue is recommended if you are breast-feeding. Below is a flexible pattern to guide you. Quantities are calculated for an average 3-3,5 kg baby. No supplementation is necessary unless your paediatrician prescribes it.

	Daytime milk feeds	Solids	Night feeds	Day sleep
2 weeks	Breast: 2-4 hourly Formula: 3-4 hourly 60-90 ml	None	3-4 hourly night feeds	45 minutes between day sleeps
5 weeks	Breast: 2-4 hourly Formula: 3-4 hourly 60-90 ml	None	2-3 night feeds	An hour of awake time between day sleeps

HAS MY BABY HAD ENOUGH?

While it is not advised to time your baby's feeds, you will probably find she will feed for 10 to 30 minutes on the first breast and 5 to 15 minutes on the second during the first week. During a feed she will drink 40 to 90 ml of milk during the first month of life. As the breast-feeding relationship continues most babies will suckle anywhere from 20 to 40 minutes during a feed. During this time, your baby will be able to eat more and more at each feed as she gains weight, and thus may be able to last longer between feeds, and drop some night feeds.

Every baby goes through **growth spurts** or frequency days when she will demand to feed more often. These usually occur at 10 to 14 days and again at six weeks. If you are breast-feeding, it is important that you allow your baby to suckle more frequently during this time, as this will help stimulate your milk production, especially in the first four weeks, to accommodate your growing baby's needs.

Formula typically takes a little longer to digest; babies who are formula-fed can therefore generally go about three hours initially without feeding again, though this may vary from baby to baby. During a growth spurt, your formula-fed baby may require an extra feed or two in a 24-hour period. This is fine, and if it continues for longer than seven days, you can increase the volume per feed.

Signs that your baby is thriving

If your baby is producing six or more wet nappies a day and gaining weight consistently, rest assured she is getting enough to eat. Breast-fed babies regain their birth weight slightly slower than bottle-fed babies but all babies should regain their birth weight by two weeks old. Other signs that your baby is thriving include filling out her newborn baby clothes, waking up for regular feeds sponta-neously, and having periods of alert interaction.

At this age you can expect your baby to gain between 120 and 250 g per week on average. If she is **consistently** gaining less than this you should be concerned, bearing in mind that she may gain only 80 g one week and 400 g the next. In this case there is not a problem.

Know your baby's signals

Follow your baby's feeding cues. If she is getting hungry she will become wakeful and may start to niggle and wriggle as she looks for nourishment. If left, she may start crying for a feed. Of course, not every cry means hunger. Sometimes your baby may simply need a clean nappy, a change of scenery or some cuddle time.

Know when your baby is full. When she stops sucking, closes her mouth or turns away from the nipple, she may be full or simply taking a break. Try burping your baby or waiting a minute before offering your breast or the bottle again. If she is ready to end the feed she will resist more vigorously.

Trust your instincts and your baby's. Parents often worry that their newborn isn't eating enough, but babies usually know just how much they need. Don't focus on how much, how often and how regularly your baby eats. Instead, look for contentment between feeds, alertness, good skin tone and steady weight gain.

SLEEPY FEEDER

Wake a sleepy feeder

Breast milk carries oxytocin, which is a sleep-inducing hormone; as a result many newborns are very sleepy feeders. If you find your newborn falls dead asleep on the breast and then wakes up hungry 30 minutes later, it is worth intervening to help her feed well. The most effective way of waking a sleepy baby is to rhythmically compress and release the breast while your baby is still latched. It also increases calorie intake by squeezing out fat molecules.

YOUR BABY'S HEALTH
Your baby's stools

Your baby will pass urine in the first 24 hours after birth and stools within the first 48 hours. Her stools are initially thick and sticky and are called meconium, changing to green, like guacamole. By the fifth day they are loose and yellow with little bits like very runny scrambled egg. From four weeks, if breast-fed, your baby can pass a stool with every nappy change or only once every three days. If you are formula feeding, your baby will pass a stool at least every second day. Do not think your baby is constipated simply because she pushes and strains to pass a stool. It is only considered constipation if your baby's stool is very hard, like small pellets.

Your baby's skin

The most common birth mark is a 'stork bite' on the forehead and the nape of the neck. This usually fades completely. Around six weeks of age your baby may develop yellow pimples on the face and the neck (infantile acne) or a yellow crusted rash in the eyebrows, on the scalp (cradle cap), behind the ears and on the face. As unsightly as this may be, just keep the skin moisturized and your baby's skin will settle within two weeks. Dry, flaky skin as well as peeling hands and feet are normal and will clear up in the first two weeks.

When using disposable nappies, do not use copious amounts of nappy cream. The nappies keep your baby's bum area dry and you will change the nappy as soon as your baby passes a stool, so nappy rashes are very unlikely.

If you see white on your baby's tongue it is due to either milk curds or thrush. White milk curds on your baby's tongue is milk residue and needs no treatment. Thrush is a fungal infection caused by *Candida albicans* and can occur in your baby's mouth and the nappy area. The mouth lesions are white and appear inside the lips and inside the cheeks. Thrush in the nappy area starts around your baby's anus and spreads up into the skin folds in red dots. You need an antifungal cream for the nappy area and an oral treatment for the mouth. Normal nappy creams do not work.

Nose and eyes

If your newborn has a blocked nose, don't be concerned as this is common and normal. Keep her nose clear by gently squirting saline down the nostrils. You may need to do this before every feed so that discomfort will not lead to poor feeding.

Tearing eyes or mucky eyes in the morning are due to blocked tear ducts. The tear ducts drain into the nose, so keeping the nose clear will help the tear ducts. Massaging the tear ducts expresses the mucus.

COMMON FEEDING ISSUES
Should I wake my newborn for feeds?

On the day your baby is born and for a few days thereafter, she will be very sleepy and may even sleep through a feed. Newborns often lose weight in the first few days after birth. Until your newborn regains her birth weight, usually within 10 to 14 days after birth, it's important to feed her at least every two to four hours during the day. This will mean occasionally waking her for a feed, especially if she has lost more than 10 per cent of her birth weight or was born prematurely or with a low birth weight. Once your newborn regains her birth-weight, settle on feeding her two- to four-hourly during the day but wait until she wakes up for a feed at night.

My bottle-fed baby only drinks small amounts of milk at a time, but wants to drink all the time. What can I do?

Although this will not cause any problems for your baby, provided she drinks enough formula in total over a 24-hour period, it can become very tiring for you to keep up with her constant demands for feeding.

- Try to encourage her to consume a little more milk with each feed by being patient. She may stop sucking to take a rest. Leave the teat in her mouth and she will most likely resume sucking. Nevertheless, one feed should last no longer than about 45 minutes.
- Encourage your baby to take greater quantities at a time by increasing the interval between feeding times. As she gets used to longer periods between feeds, she will also take more milk.
- A bottle-fed baby can be guided into a regular feeding pattern.

My breasts are sore, painful and engorged. What can I do for the pain?

During the early days of breast-feeding, your breasts may become too full or engorged because your body has not yet worked out how much milk to produce for efficient feeding. In addition, since you are feeding on cue, your body has no idea exactly when the next feed is and so produces milk preemptively. To manage engorged breasts:

- Feed regularly in the first weeks to prevent engorgement.
- Ensure your baby drains your breasts at each feed.
- If your breasts are too full for your baby to latch with ease, hand express a small amount of milk before the feed, which will soften your breasts, making you more comfortable and latching easier. If you do use an expressing pump, be sure not to express too much before your baby feeds.
- If you are very uncomfortable, use a warm cloth on your breasts before feeding or expressing. The warmth will bring relief and you will be able to feed or express a little milk with greater ease.
- Keep a cabbage in the fridge. Remove the outer leaves, wash, pat dry and make a hole in the middle for your nipple. Crush slightly and place them in your bra. The thinking behind this is that cabbage contains ingredients that improve the blood flow in and out of the breast area, allowing the body to reabsorb the fluid trapped in the breasts, thereby relieving the engorgement. Leave on for 20 minutes at a time every two hours.
- If the cabbage remedy does not appeal to you, use a cold bag or cool flannel for 20 minutes every two hours.
- Within a few days your breasts should settle.

Engorged breasts are painful to the touch but after a feed the pain dissipates. If your breasts are tender and sore after a feed you may have a blocked duct or even mastitis.

I have been breast-feeding for ten days and my nipples are a source of agony. I don't know if I can continue feeding.

Usually tenderness occurs in the first few days and peaks at around three to six days of feeding as your nipples are not used to the wear and tear of a baby's sucking. To limit tenderness and damage:

- Ensure your baby is latched properly and sucking correctly – seek help from clinic sister or lactation consultant in case she has difficulty sucking due to tongue tie (see page 65).
- Wash your nipples with water only as soap can be very drying.
- Air-dry your nipples after each feed and replace damp nursing pads frequently.

If your nipples continue to be very sensitive and you experience a shooting pain while your baby feeds, you may have nipple thrush. This is caused by *Candida albicans* and is easily treated by your GP.

CHAPTER 11

Simple feeding sense from six to 17 weeks

Your little one is six weeks old and growing by the day. You may find that this holds great ambivalence for you as you yearn to hold on to those newborn days but find yourself wishing away the challenge of a colicky baby and sleep deprivation. On the feeding side you may find that you are settling into it and your feeding choice, be it breast or bottle, is working well for you.

WHAT TO EXPECT IN TERMS OF FEEDING AT THIS STAGE

- Breast milk supply is established and you should be **breast-feeding** with more confidence.
- You can guide your baby towards a **three- to four-hour feed rhythm,** but be flexible – he is still little. Be sure not to let more than four hours pass between day feeds.
- Expect a **growth spurt** or frequency days at six weeks and again at four months. If you feed your baby more frequently during these days he will be satisfied and content.
- If you are **bottle feeding**, your baby will start to feed less frequently and will drink larger volumes (90-180 ml) four to five times in 24 hours.
- Your baby may sleep for one longer stretch of six to eight hours at **night** without waking for a feed and wake three- to four-hourly thereafter.
- Your breast-fed baby may need **cluster feeds** in the early evening. If he is unsettled when you put him down, he may settle well with a top-up breast-feed or a bottle of expressed breast milk or formula.
- Milk provides all the nutrition your baby needs at this stage. Do not consider **solids** during this stage. Introducing solids when your baby is this young may increase the risk of allergies and obesity later in life.

WHAT YOUR BABY IS UP TO
Development

Your little one is growing up and is able to **hold his head up** with increasing success although it is not yet fully stable. His primitive sucking and tongue thrust reflexes still predominate and this indicates that he is not yet ready for solids.

Your baby will become more alert as the weeks progress, start to coo and develop a social **smile**, so there will probably be more interaction between you and him during feeds. He begins to associate activities with actions, for instance if you turn him on his side into the feeding position he will expect a feed and start rooting for the breast.

Sleep

At this age your baby can manage awake times of 60 to 80 minutes before needing a sleep. Remember to act on his awake times and signals and you will find a pattern of **day sleeps** will start to emerge at last. Depending on the length of his sleeps, your baby will be having in the region of three to four sleeps during the day. Encourage this pattern by being consistent (same place, same time) and repeating it each day. Your baby's **bedtime** should be no later than 7 pm and should be preceded by a quiet, calm feed in a dim room.

Colic and stimulation

Colic and early infant crying peaks at six weeks and by 12 weeks, any colicky patches are likely to be a thing of the past. You are also getting to know your little one's signals as he now has different cries for hunger and tiredness. Before assuming your baby is hungry, take time to read his signals when he is crying in case he is simply overtired or overstimulated. Hiccups, for instance, are often associated with digestive issues but more often they are a sign of overstimulation. Likewise, blue around the mouth may not indicate a gas but rather a change of state as your baby copes with too much stimuli.

FEEDING YOUR SIX TO 17 WEEK BABY

During the first four months, milk will **provide all the nutrition** your baby needs. You can expect your baby to consume more milk during each feed, so he won't need to feed as often and will sleep longer at night.

Breast-feeding

If your baby is still very unsettled, do not automatically think your milk supply is low or that your baby is not tolerating your breast milk well. Almost all babies do better on breast milk than formula milk. Swapping to formula feeds now will in all likelihood not make for a more settled baby. In fact, the opposite may be true. If your baby is unsettled and colicky consider the following before introducing formula:

- *Is he overstimulated and overtired and suffering from normal three-month colic?* In this case, a regular day sleep routine may really help to settle your baby. He should not be awake for more than 60 to 90 minutes before being settled to sleep during the day.
- *Does he have reflux?* If your baby posits a lot and is very unsettled after feeds and unhappy when put down for sleep or held in the horizontal feeding position, he may have reflux. Some babies suffer from reflux without positing at all. If you suspect your baby is suffering from reflux speak to your doctor. Also see page 56.

SENSE-ABLE FEEDING
As impossible as it may seem, lie down for a nap for at least one of your baby's day sleeps. This will be good for your sanity and your milk supply in the early evening.

- *Is your milk supply sufficient?* It is hard to trust you have enough breast milk as breasts are not calibrated and you cannot gauge how much your baby has ingested. If you think that you baby is not getting enough milk (see page 122 on how to determine if your baby is getting enough breast milk), it is worth working on increasing your milk supply before supplementing your baby's diet with formula milk. Expressing during the day and offering a top-up of the expressed milk in the evening when your milk supply may be a little low is often a good solution.

INCREASING MILK SUPPLY

It is tempting to move your baby onto formula in an attempt to meet his nutritional needs and have him sleep better at night if you feel your milk supply is dwindling at this stage. If you value breast-feeding, it is worth making an effort at this stage to bump up your milk supply.

- **Eat well:** You may have neglected yourself and your own nutrition. See page 24 for a healthy meal plan for breast-feeding. Eat regular meals and ensure you are getting a range of nutrients from all the food groups: fresh fruit and vegetables, protein, starches and healthy fats like olive oil and avocado.
- **Drink enough**: Have some liquid at each feed and an additional two glasses at other times to ensure adequate intake of fluids. This can be water, Rooibos tea or Jungle Juice:
  - 50 ml blackthorn berry tonic (Schlehen's elixir)
  - 1 litre apple, berry or grape juice
  - 2 litres water
  - 1 sachet fruit-flavoured Rehydrate solution (from pharmacy)
  - 1 Cal-C-vita tablet and a few drops of rescue remedy to help you relax (optional)
- **Don't overschedule your life:** Make sure there is time in your schedule to relax and to rest.
- **Feed more frequently:** For a few days you may need to feed more frequently to increase your breast milk supply.
- **Feed in a calm space:** Babies at this age are more likely to get distracted and stop feeding at the slightest disturbance, which means your breasts are stimulated for a shorter time.
- **Remain on your supplement**: A good supplement includes all the nutrients present in your prenatal multivitamin, including calcium and iron. Remain on your prenatal supplement during breast-feeding.
- **Prescribed medication:** Your doctor may prescribe medication such as Sulpiride or Metoclopramide to increase your milk supply.

Bottle feeding

Many moms have to go back to work after their maternity leave – usually when their baby is between three and six months old. If your baby is breast-fed you can either express breast milk to feed him when you are not there, or you can switch to formula. Some babies make the transition without batting an eye whereas others need a little more patience to get through it. (See Chapter 3, page 40 for weaning onto bottles.)

At this age you may also choose to supplement your baby's breast milk diet with formula. Whatever your reason, and whether the transition is partial or complete, introducing formula need not be a daunting experience.

When choosing a first milk it is best to begin with a normal cow's milk based formula unless your baby has eczema or mom or dad is allergic. (See page 37 for a comprehensive guide to formulas.) You can expect your baby to drink between 450 and 900 ml in a day. Every baby is an individual, though, so as long as your baby is thriving and gaining weight, do not worry if he drinks less than the suggested volume on the formula tin for his age.

If your baby seems unsettled it is probably more to do with overstimulation and tiredness than the wrong formula choice. Resist the temptation to swap formulas simply because your baby is fractious. If he shows signs of a formula intolerance such as excessive gas, diarrhoea (which may be bloody), spitting up, vomiting, and poor weight gain, you need to consult with your healthcare provider before changing his milk.

> **SENSE-ABLE FEEDING**
> Your baby's digestive tract is not mature enough to cope with solid foods at this stage. Solids now could make him more susceptible to digestive problems like celiac disease and increase the risk of allergic eczema.

Supplements

At this age additional supplements, water, juice and solid foods aren't usually necessary.

A HEALTHY MEAL PLAN FOR YOUR SIX TO 17 WEEK-OLD BABY

Guide your baby into a flexible feeding routine.

- When he cries, listen to his cry and consider how long it has been since he was last fed. If three or more hours have passed, feed him. Do not be rigid about having him wait longer.
- Provided your baby is gaining weight, do not offer a feed if less than two and a half hours have passed since the last feed. Ask yourself if he could be tired (80 minutes since his last sleep) or if he needs to be calmed after some stimulation – take a walk, swaddle him in a cotton blanket or place him in a baby sling or pouch to keep him close to you. **Stretch** the interval by encouraging non-nutritive hand-to-mouth or dummy sucking and by gently rocking and soothing him.
- If he is still fussy after this time, feed him as he may be experiencing a growth spurt (at six weeks and at 17 weeks). By reading your baby's signals and meeting his needs, you help him learn to feel secure and trust you.

Your baby's flexible routine at this stage can look something like this:

	Daytime milk feeds	Solid food	Night feeds	Day sleep
6 weeks	Breast: 2½–4 hourly Formula: 3½–4 hourly 90–180 ml	None	Two night feeds – one just before midnight and one before 4 am	One hour between day sleeps
17 weeks	Breast: 3–4 hourly Formula: 4 hourly 90–180 ml	None	First night feed drops and baby has one feed around 1 am and another at around 5 am	One and a half hours between day sleeps

HAS MY BABY HAD ENOUGH?

The flexible schedule in the previous paragraph is a general guideline. Your baby may be hungrier more or less often than this, so it's important to pay attention to his signals of being hungry or full. When he has had enough, he may slow down, stop, or turn away from the breast or bottle. As he is getting older, your baby may start to feed less frequently and sleep for longer periods at night. You can be reassured that he is getting enough if he:

• seems alert, content and active
• is steadily gaining weight, growing and developing
• feeds five to seven times per day
• has six to eight wet nappies in 24 hours

If your baby doesn't appear satisfied, even after feeding, and cries constantly or is irritable, he may not be getting enough. Call your baby's doctor if you are concerned.

During periods of rapid growth, you may notice that your little one wants to feed more frequently. If you are breast-feeding, frequent feeds prompt your body to increase the milk supply. Supply and demand will get into balance within a few days. If you are bottle feeding you may need to offer your baby more milk at a time and feed him more frequently during the day.

Weight gain

Your baby's weight gain slows down to 100-200 g per week. Most babies will double their birth weight by four to five months of age.

YOUR BABY'S HEALTH
Stools
From about six weeks, breast-fed babies tend to have fewer bowel movements than they did before. When your baby is around two months old, he may not have a bowel movement after each feed, or even every day. Call your doctor if your breast-fed baby hasn't had a bowel movement after seven days, and if your formula-fed baby has not had a bowel movement after three days.

Teething
From three months of age babies start to drool and put everything they grasp into their mouth. They do this because they can and they are exploring their environment and experiencing new tastes and textures. It is not because they are teething or because they are hungry and ready for solids.

Skin
Your baby may still battle with a rash on his neck and face (infantile acne) until about eight weeks of age and it is common for babies of this age to get heat rashes from being overdressed. Take care not to dress your baby too warmly in cold weather as he may perspire under all the layers of clothing.

Unsettled or sick
Babies cry more at around six weeks of age than at any other time. This is generally not a sign that your baby is sick or that his milk needs to be changed or that he needs colic medication. Try not to use medication except as prescribed by your doctor if there is a definite medical problem.

If your baby is still mainly at home, he is probably not being exposed to all the viruses that cause respiratory tract infections. If he does get sick it may be more serious than if he had had time to build up his immunity. If your young baby develops a fever he must be seen by a doctor on the same day. Antibodies from the womb, in colostrum and from breast milk are still protecting your baby.

Vaccination
Most babies have very little or no adverse reaction after vaccination, and this should not affect your baby's feeding at all. If he is fractious after a visit to the clinic, it is most likely from overstimulation.

COMMON FEEDING ISSUES

How do I know if my baby is going through a growth spurt and what should I do?

Babies go through several growth spurts or frequency days in the first year, which accounts for the dramatic growth between birth and a year. The first occurs between seven and ten days, followed by one at six weeks, four months, six months and nine months. These ages are approximate, and your baby may have a growth spurt at other times as well.

Your baby may be having a growth spurt in this age band if:

- He demands three to four breast-feeds in six hours.
- He finishes his bottle of formula and seems to want more within an hour.
- He was on a regular three-hour schedule, and suddenly he wants to feed more frequently.
- He no longer sleeps for such long stretches at night. He may have finally started sleeping for a long stretch during the night, only to start waking again several times, seemingly ravenous. Although your baby may not yet have a fixed sleeping routine, any changes in the pattern may indicate a growth spurt.
- He begins waking early from naps – if he previously napped one to two hours or longer at a stretch and is suddenly waking up after only 30-45 minutes and seems hungry.

MANAGING GROWTH SPURTS

Take the pressure off yourself and don't schedule anything for a day or two so you can focus on feeding your baby, then do so when he demands to be fed.

If you are breast-feeding, build up your milk supply by drinking enough fluids and eating the right food (see page 24).

HOW LONG DO THEY LAST?

Growth spurts typically last only two to three days, but can sometimes last for a week or longer. If the growth spurt lasts a week or longer, make sure you are drinking enough and consuming enough calories to compensate for the additional feeds. You may feel hungrier than usual when your baby is going through a growth spurt.

How can I encourage my seven week-old baby to drink from a bottle if he refuses?

Your baby may be refusing the bottle because he does not like the new shape and feel of a teat or he may dislike the taste of formula milk. You should offer a bottle by six weeks of age and then one every two weeks or so, even if you plan to exclusively breast-feed for a year or more. This is so that your baby becomes accustomed to the feel of the bottle, in case of an emergency when you are not around to feed or if you are going back to work. Try these suggestions if he refuses to take the bottle:

- Get someone else to offer it
- Offer it at a time when your baby is neither starving nor completely full
- Feed him away from where you usually sit, so that he does not anticipate getting a breast-feed
- Try a different brand of teat – for some reason a latex 'Curity' shaped teat seems to work well for babies who refuse the bottle
- Leave the house so your partner can persevere without you interfering.

My 12 week-old breast-fed baby appears disinterested in feeding. How do I manage this?

The taste of your breast milk may change if you have your period or are taking medication. If you are not well, you may have less milk. Continue to express to keep up your milk supply.

Your baby may be unwell with a blocked nose or a sore throat. As he grows older he may also be easily distracted by activities or noise around him. Use a feeding shawl or feed your baby in a quiet space with reduced sensory input.

Anxiety on your part will aggravate the problem, so stay calm and ask for help if needed. Create a relaxed environment for you and the baby and rest assured that this is generally a short-term problem.

My ten week-old baby has white spots inside his mouth and won't feed. Is this thrush?

Thrush is a yeast or fungal infection caused by Candida. Most babies will have this yeast on or in their bodies by the time they are six months old and in the vast majority of cases it does us no harm and we don't even notice it's there. It forms part of the billions of microorganisms that live and thrive in our body and form part of our immune system.

Feeding difficulties associated with a thrush infection in a baby's mouth are rare, but can occur if the infection is severe. If your baby has oral thrush, there's a chance that he may also develop a yeast infection on his little bottom, because the yeast can pass from his mouth through his gastro-intestinal tract.

IDENTIFYING THRUSH
- *White or cream-coloured patches* like milk curds on the roof of his mouth, inside his cheeks and on his tongue. These may be surrounded by red areas.
- His entire tongue may have a *solid white coating*; don't mistake milk residue as thrush. Milk residue on the tongue is quite thin and usually wipes off easily, whereas thrush does not.

PREVENTING AND TREATING THRUSH
- Ensure all bottles and nipples are washed thoroughly and sterilised. Wipe the inside of your baby's mouth with a cotton wool pad to help remove the milk from his mouth after a feed. Milk residue encourages the growth of thrush.

- Clean your baby's hands frequently with soap and water.
- Consult your healthcare practitioner with regards to oral medication to treat the thrush if your baby is fussing and feeding is affected.

I think I have thrush on my nipples. How do I treat it and prevent it from happening again?

Thrush can cause nipple pain, which may only start 15-20 minutes after the feed. Your nipples will be sensitive, slightly sore and itchy. Thrush may be triggered if you are on antibiotics, are run down, tired or unwell. Your baby may have thrush and transfer it to you. Prevent and treat it as follows:

- Wash your hands in soapy water before and after going to the toilet, changing nappies and breast-feeding.
- Soak your baby's clothes and your underwear in nappy bleach powder. Wash in hot water and dry in the sun.
- Air-dry your nipples after each feed and expose them to the sun for a few minutes each day.
- Change breast pads after each feed and avoid using breast pads with a plastic backing.
- Eat a nutritious diet including yogurt with live AB culture and get lots of rest.
- Consult with your doctor or clinic sister. Follow the recommended treatment as prescribed for up to two weeks after symptoms have gone.
- Treat your baby's mouth and, if necessary, his bottom with an antifungal cream recommended by your doctor.

Is my milk sustaining my three month-old baby?
He wakes once at night to feed.

If your baby is only waking once at night, your milk is definitely sustaining him. You can expect in the next few weeks for your baby to start waking a little more at night as he starts to need extra milk to sustain his growth.

My baby of 13 weeks cannot be stretched longer than three hours between feeds. Should I be stretching him to four hours?

Remember, all babies are different and your baby may be one of those who prefer smaller feeds more frequently. Feeding your baby three- to four-hourly is completely acceptable.

CHAPTER 12

Simple feeding sense for your four to six month-old

Your little one has really turned the corner now. She is more settled and loves to interact and you are more proficient at reading her needs and moods. In addition she can now interpret her own body signals much better and is able to self-soothe or communicate with a specific cry when she has a need that requires intervention.

Between four and six months, she will start to show signs that she is ready for solids, so just when everything is starting to feel manageable, you will be faced with the next big question of infancy: "When do I introduce solids?" This is probably one of the more challenging and controversial decisions you will have to make. Use your common sense and intuition when sifting through the available information, then make your decision, stick to it and focus on enjoying this exciting phase.

WHAT TO EXPECT IN TERMS OF FEEDING AT THIS STAGE

- Your **milk supply** will be well established at this stage and you will be breast-feeding your baby four to six times in 24 hours – aim to feed her three and a half to four hourly during the day.
- Expect a **growth spurt** at four months and respond by feeding more frequently for 24 to 48 hours. Your milk supply will **increase on demand**.
- Your **bottle-fed** baby will start to feed less frequently and will drink larger volumes (120-240 ml) four to five times in 24 hours by six months. If your bottle-fed baby does not increase the volume or frequency of feeds, starting solids will be important.
- At some point during this stage, your baby will appear **hungrier**, not stretch for as long between feeds and will wake more frequently at night. To satisfy her growing appetite, you will need to have her spend longer at the breast, feed her more frequently, increase the amount of formula you feed her, or introduce solids.

WHAT YOUR BABY IS UP TO
Development

Your baby's **head control** improves dramatically at this stage. She can hold her head up and by six months sits supported on your lap. This head and neck control is vital for moving her onto the next stage of feeding. She will start to **reach** intentionally for objects and delights in getting her hands on things and putting them to her mouth.

Between four and six months of age the **tongue-thrust reflex** that helps to protect your baby from choking diminishes. In some babies it disappears rapidly and in others it takes a while. If you introduce solids before this reflex is fully integrated, you will find your baby's tongue will push the food from her mouth. If there are other signs that your baby is ready for solids you can introduce them before this reflex is fully integrated.

By now your baby reads her own internal messages well enough to know when she is hungry while you will likewise have learnt to interpret her hunger signals.

Sleep

> **SENSE-ABLE FEEDING**
> Do not interpret the tongue-thrust reflex in action as an indication that your baby dislikes certain foods or is hesitant to explore new textures.

Your baby can cope with being **awake** for 90 to 120 minutes at a time, which is when you will need to feed and stimulate her. She should sleep for three to five hours during the day divided into three or four sleeps, and for 10 to 12 hours at night with one night waking. This will amount to a total of 14 to 18 hours sleep in a 24-hour cycle.

FEEDING YOUR FOUR TO SIX MONTH-OLD
Breast-feeding

The composition of your breast milk changes all the time to meet your baby's nutritional needs. At some point your milk will no longer meet all these needs and your baby will require solids. Try to continue breast-feeding so while introducing solids as this offers a protective effect on your baby's digestive system.

Your body has recovered from the birth and you are probably feeling more energetic, more confident as a mom and may start to socialise more frequently. You and your baby will start to get out more and life gets busier. Your baby is alert and loves interacting with the world around her. She is stronger and sucks faster and also finds life very interesting. For all these reasons, feeds become much shorter and possibly a little disrupted. Feeding and developing a routine become more challenging as you work towards finding a healthy medium between 'getting on' with life and feeding your baby according to a schedule.

Coping with changing nutritional needs

Just when you get used to enjoying a longer stretch of sleep at night, your baby may start waking earlier, with a shorter stretch between feeds at night. Instead of sleeping from 7 pm to after midnight, she may start waking before midnight again. She may also be less settled during the day and you may be told she is having a growth spurt.

If you have chosen to breast-feed exclusively until close to six months, you need to adjust your sleep expectations and breast-feed your baby at night. This will result in a more content baby as well as increase your breast milk supply. (See page 120 for advice on increasing your milk supply.)

Weaning your baby from breast to bottle

While it is best to continue breast-feeding while introducing solids, this is an age when many moms decide to replace breast-feeds with infant formula or to top up or supplement their baby's diet with expressed breast milk. Switching to bottles can be done in part or fully. You may be going back to work and breast-feed in the morning and evening and feed formula or expressed breast milk during the day. Or you may choose to stop breast-feeding and offer your baby only formula from now on.

It is advisable to make a gradual change if you have been breast-feeding. Where possible, reduce the number of feeds according to your level of comfort. This may mean replacing one feed per day for a week with formula. It is helpful to have someone else offer the bottle. As your baby gets more accustomed to formula or breast milk from a bottle, you can feed her yourself again. (See page 40 for details on weaning from breast to bottle.)

Give your baby lots of cuddles and hugs when she is not hungry to satisfy the sensory and emotional benefits of breast-feeding. Offer her the bottle at the first signs of hunger, not when she is already starving – you don't want her upset and anxious. Some babies take to the bottle more easily than others; just persevere and your little one will eventually take to this new way of feeding. Remember that breast-fed babies tend to ingest smaller amounts more frequently, so she might prefer a similar pattern initially when moving onto the bottle.

Formula

Today's formulas will meet your baby's nutritional needs very effectively. However, the taste and composition of formula differs from that of breast milk and your baby has to get used to it. If at first she appears to not like the formula, or is unsettled with winds and even constipation, don't just switch to another formula.

CHOOSING A FORMULA

Use a good cow's milk-based formula unless your baby has eczema or her mom or dad is allergic, in which case she should be on an elemental formula. (See page 37 for details.)

As your baby reaches six months, move her onto a stage-two or follow-on formula. If she gets constipated when you do, you can leave her on newborn formula as she will probably get extra nutrients from solids.

Bottle feeding quantities

Formula feeding recommendations are based on your baby's age and approximate weight for her age. Remember, your baby is unique and may weigh more or less than the average baby of the same age. In addition, all babies have different levels of energy and some babies use more energy than others. Together, these factors determine how much milk she requires.

Use this as a general guide for feeds, milk quantities and day sleeps in 24 hours:

Age	Daytime milk feeds	Solid meals	Night feeds	Day sleep
4 months	Breast: 3-4 hourly Formula: 4 hourly during the day, 120–150 ml	None or introducing mid-morning then mid-afternoon	One or two night feeds	One and a half hours between day sleeps
5 months	Breast: 3-4 hourly Formula: 4 hourly during the day, 150–180 ml	Introduce solids: up to three meals in a day	One night feed after midnight and an early morning feed between 4 and 6 am	One and a half to two hours between sleeps
6 months	Breast: 4 hourly Formula: 4 feeds a day, 150-240 ml	Three meals a day with protein beginning to be introduced	May begin to sleep through or have one night feed at around 1 am, then early morning at 5 am	Two hours between sleeps – three or four sleeps a day

SENSE-ABLE FEEDING
Your prem baby has specific nutritional needs and you need to feed her according to her corrected age. If she was born at 30 weeks gestation (ten weeks early), subtract ten weeks from her age. Effectively if she is six months old, her corrected age is only 14 weeks and she may not be ready for solids. (See table on page 108 for introducing solids to a prem baby.)

Your baby will need to continue breast or formula feeding for the duration of the first year. As she grows and starts eating solids, whether she is on breast milk or formula, she will naturally reduce the number of milk feeds.

Introducing solids

The latest information and research on the best time to introduce solids is discussed at length in Chapter 4 (see page 42).

To recap, when solids are introduced too early, that is before **17 weeks** of age, the immaturity of your baby's digestive and immune systems may increase her risk of developing an allergy. This risk increases if you baby already has eczema or you or her dad (not siblings or other family members) is allergic (see Chapter 6 page 68).

The best age for your baby to begin eating solids will depend on both physical and emotional factors. She needs to be physically ready as well as emotionally ready to deal with solids. You will sense whether or not your baby is ready to eat solids. Learn to trust this intuitive side of being a parent.

Your baby is physically ready for the introduction of solids if she
- Is between four and six months old
- Can hold up her head
- Sits comfortably with support
- Is no longer satisfied with just milk feeds even if volume is at an age-appropriate level
- Is unsettled between feeds during the day and wants to feed more often than three-hourly
- Is demanding more frequent milk feeds at night or suddenly starts waking closer to midnight again
- Is not gaining weight adequately
- Shows diminished tongue-thrust reflex.

Your baby is emotionally ready for the introduction of solids if she
- Starts to show an interest in foods
- Watches you and turns her head towards you while you are eating
- Mirrors your mouth movements by opening her mouth in response to your eating
- Shows excitement when watching others eat

It is critical to start introducing solids by six months of age even if some of these signs are not present. Babies are born with a store of nutrients that will normally be adequate for the first few months of life. Iron is one example. After the first four to six months your baby's iron stores begin to deplete and milk is no longer an adequate sole source of iron, so you need to give your baby additional iron-rich foods.

Another reason not to delay introducing solids after six months is that there is a window period when babies are more receptive to new tastes and flavours. Delaying or restricting the introduction of the food experience can result in a lazy and fussy eater.

First foods

Introduce one to two food types at a time to give your baby a day or two to adjust to the new food. Foods to try between four and months:
- Rice cereal
- Quinoa porridge
- Maize cereal
- Maltabella porridge
- First veggie mix: baby marrow, gem squash, sweet potato
- Orange vegetables: butternut, carrots, pumpkin, sweet potato, Hubbard squash, potato
- Green veggie mix: spinach, baby marrow, gem squash, peas, beans
- Fruit: apples, pears, peaches, prunes, papino, avocado, banana, mango, melon.

SENSE-ABLE FEEDING
In this early stage of solid introduction where your baby is the learner and you are the teacher, breast or formula milk should still make up the bulk of her nutritional intake.

A good first meal could be one heaped teaspoon of single-grain baby cereal mixed with expressed breast or formula milk. This will make up about three teaspoons of porridge. Or try three teaspoons of puréed first veggies (gem squash, sweet potato and baby marrow) mixed with milk.

RICE CEREAL OR VEGGIES?	Rice cereal as a first food	Reasons to start with veggies
	• It is relatively bland in taste • You can mix it to a thin consistency • It provides necessary iron • It is believed to be relatively hypo-allergenic.	• Some babies don't like the bland taste of rice cereal and never take enthusiastically, particularly closer to 6 months of age • Rice cereal may cause constipation; vegetables and fruit have large amounts of soluble fibre to sort out any tummy trouble.

A good time of day

Introduce the first solid meal at a time of day when your baby is happily awake, in the calm-alert state. Choose a time of day when you are not stressed. A good time is in the morning, about an hour after a milk feed and during play time. Making the first food experiences fun and stimulating will set the tone for many happy feeding times.

Four steps to solids

STEP 1

Offer your baby 1-3 teaspoons of the chosen food mid-morning. Gradually increase the amount and adjust the consistency according to how she tolerates it. If your baby is not yet five months, stick to this step for up to a week. If your baby is older than five months, progress to the next step after three days.

STEP 2

Add a second feed in the late afternoon between 4 and 5 pm. Offer a mix of *first veggies* mixed smooth with a little milk. Do this for about a week if your baby is not yet five months, or for three days if your baby is older than five months before moving on to the next step.

STEP 3

Move the morning solid feed to around 12 noon, after the mid-morning milk feed, as a lunch. Offer the *first veggie mix* at this time. Your baby will now be having vegetables for lunch and supper and it is time to introduce a breakfast meal of a porridge or cereal. Offer porridge like Maltabella or rice/maize cereal after the morning milk feed. You can also add some fruit into your baby's diet.

Start by adding half a teaspoon of puréed fruit to her cereal breakfast, and offer dessert of 1-2 teaspoons of puréed fruit after her lunch and supper. Your baby is now having three solid meals a day and four-hourly milk feeds. Continue to introduce the recommended foods one by one until she is eating a varied diet. When she is close to six months and has been on solids for 3-4 weeks, move on to Step 4.

STEP 4

As long as your baby does not have an allergy to cow's milk protein, you can now start introducing some natural full-cream yogurt with any one meal of the day. Mix it into the cereal/fruit breakfast or into the vegetables or fruit at lunch and dinner.

A HEALTHY MEAL PLAN (SEE RECIPES, PAGES 160-168)

4-5 MONTHS

INTRODUCE: Rice cereal, first veggie mix		
Week 1	Mid-morning	1-3 t cereal or first veggie mix
Week 2 until your baby is 5 months old, then go to week 2 of the next plan	Midday	1-3 t cereal or first veggie mix
	Evening	1-3 t first veggie mix before bath and bedtime

OVER 5 MONTHS

Week 1	INTRODUCE: Rice cereal, first veggie mix		
	Day 1-3	Mid-morning	1-3 t cereal or first veggie mix
	Day 4-7	Midday	1-3 t cereal or first veggie mix
		Evening	1-3 t of first veggie mix before bath and bedtime feed
Week 2	INTRODUCE: 1. Porridge: Cereal or maltabella 2. Fruit: Jarred or fresh apple purée, pear, prunes, mango 3. Orange veggies		
	Day 1-3	8-9 am	2-3 t porridge at breakfast plus 1 t apple purée
		Midday	3-6 t orange veggie mix
		4-5 pm	3-6 t first veggie mix
	Day 4-7	8-9 am	Offer 3-6 t cereal with 3 t fruit: pear, apple, prune, mango
		Midday	Offer 3-6 t vegetables, then 1-2 t puréed fruit
		4-5 pm	Offer 3-6 t vegetables, then 1-2 t puréed fruit

Week 3	INTRODUCE: 1. Oats porridge 2. Maize porridge (mieliepap) 3. Yogurt, full-cream 4. Cream cheese, plain	
	Breakfast	3-6 t cereal, alternating the cereals plus 3 t fruit
	Lunch	3-6 t first/orange veg + 2 t yogurt
	Supper	3-6 t first/orange veg mix + 2 t cream cheese
Week 4–6 or until age 6 months	Continue as week 3 but increase meal quantity to 3–12 t in total	

TIPS FOR INTRODUCING SOLIDS	Let your baby touch and feel the food from the first day of solids. This will make her more receptive to trying the new foods.

TIPS FOR INTRODUCING SOLIDS

Let your baby touch and feel the food from the first day of solids. This will make her more receptive to trying the new foods.

- Add breast or formula milk to the vegetables before you liquidize; this makes the mix smoother and adds some protein to a vegetable meal.
- Ensure your baby's sitting position is comfortable.
- Use a small, soft, flat spoon for feeding.
- Hold the spoon in front of your baby's mouth as a cue to eat.
- As you take the spoon to her mouth, open your mouth so that she can copy your action.
- Place the spoon on the top of her tongue so that the food touches her top lip, making swallowing easier.
- If she is unhappy, stop feeding immediately – do not force-feed her.
- Provide her with positive feedback when she tastes some food, for example: 'That tastes yummy', 'is the porridge nice and sweet?' 'Yum, Mommy loves apples too …' Don't use accolades like 'clever girl, good girl' to avoid food being linked to performance rather than enjoyment.
- It is not a problem to skip a day or two in the early days of introducing solids. It is more important that the environment remains relaxed and stress free.

HAS MY BABY HAD ENOUGH?

At this stage feeding your baby is all about the learning experience. Use the guidelines in the meal plan and look out for the signals that your baby gives you as to how much she wants. Signals that she is full could include: turning her head away, closing her lips tightly or even crying.

Your baby is having enough nutrition in a day if she is:

- Breast-feeding 4-5 times per day
- Drinking sufficient formula milk (600-900 ml a day)
- Content after a feed
- Producing more than 6-8 wet nappies in 24 hours

Your baby's thirst will ensure that she keeps drinking enough milk in a day to get all her nutrients. Don't allow her to fill up on water or even juice in a bottle – this will spoil her appetite for milk. Only offer 30 ml of water in a bottle after solids if needed.

Like adults, babies have different appetites and energy levels. "Some babies love to eat, others eat to live." You will find that everybody has an opinion on *how much* your baby should eat. This can be very confusing and anxiety provoking if your baby's intake does not match up to some or other 'ideal'. Be aware of information overload and remember your baby is an individual. Her health, happiness and energy level will indicate whether she is getting enough to eat.

Weight gain

You can expect your baby to gain 100-140 g per week, but all babies grow at their own pace according to their own growth curve. Weight loss is a concern and needs to be addressed by your healthcare provider.

YOUR BABY'S HEALTH
Constipation

As solids are introduced, **constipation** can become a problem. Constipation refers to the passing of a very hard stool or little pellets, usually only once every two or three days, causing your baby to strain terribly. To deal with this problem, make sure she is drinking sufficient fluids. In addition to the milk allocation for the day, she may need 50-100 ml of water.

Introduce foods that are known to help the tummy work. Prunes are well known for this and can be given as fruit purée or 5 ml of juice mixed into 30 ml of water after a meal. Strained oats porridge is also great for getting her tummy to work. If constipation continues, use a liquid containing lactulose (e.g. syrups like Duphalac, Laxette and Lacson). These are not harmful and work in the same way as prunes but should only be used on the advice of your health-care provider.

Rashes

It is common for children to develop a rash around the mouth or on the body when they start to eat solid food. This does not mean that your baby is allergic. If the reaction is a mild rash, be sure to try that food again before even considering that it was an allergy.

COMMON FEEDING ISSUES

My four month-old refuses to take the bottle and I am going back to work. What should I do?

Take a breath, stand back and assess the situation.

- Are you offering the bottle when your baby is not sufficiently hungry? It is much more likely to be successful if she is hungry.
- Try offering the bottle and then giving her a short break to play. After 20 minutes try again.
- Try asking someone else to give her the bottle – she might be picking up on your anxiety or the smell of your breast milk. Go for a walk or run some errands to get out of the house.
- Check that the environment is calm and that there are no distractions.
- Try a different feeding position or different feeding environment.

Also read page 40 on weaning from breast to bottle for more information.

How do I choose a starter cereal?

As this will be one of your baby's first foods, you will be justifiably concerned about what the cereal contains. If your baby has a diagnosed cow's milk protein and/or soya allergy or a history of eczema or allergies in Mom or Dad, avoid any cereal with dairy or soya protein. Make sure the cereal is sugar-free and free from preservatives. If you can afford it, an organic, single-grain dairy-free cereal is probably the best choice. Simple and affordable and just as good an option is a single-grain porridge such as Maltabella or maize porridge (mieliepap).

I lead a very busy life and have little time to cook for my baby. How bad is convenience baby food?

The benefits of cooking for your baby are significant. Not only is it less expensive, but home-cooked food has more taste and enlists baby's taste buds in an exciting journey of exploring food. The texture of homecooked food is seldom as smooth as that of bottled versions and babies eating home-cooked food tend to progress to more adventurous textures with greater ease. Home cooking enables you to include your family tastes and favourites in your baby's diet from an early age, which will assist the transition to modified family meals. The only negative is time, but bear in mind that your baby eats very small portions in the beginning so you could cook up a batch of food and freeze for future use (see page 160 for recipes and freezing suggestions), which brings you back to convenience.

Bottled convenience foods are easy to store and take with you when you are away from home. Unfortunately their flavour is limited and textures often go from very smooth to very lumpy, which may offend a baby just getting used to solid foods. Use bottled foods for emergencies and quick meals over weekends only. There are also ready-made baby meals available privately or in stores, that are fresh and tasty. You can buy and freeze these foods for those days when you just don't get around to cooking.

My baby has gone off her milk since starting solids. What must I do?

At this stage milk is still a very important part of your baby's diet. She may be drinking less milk if solid food is given immediately before milk feeds and fill her up too much. In addition, you may be offering your baby too much at each meal (see page 133 for guidelines). Your expectations regarding the amount of milk she should have may be unrealistic. A baby who is eating solids only needs 600-900 ml milk per day, of which up to 30% can be incorporated into the solids. To address the problem, cut back on the amount of solid food you are offering to fit in with our guidelines, and make sure that there is at least a two-hour gap between solids and milk feeds.

If your baby still refuses to drink more milk and really prefers her solids, you can mix her milk with solids and even add an extra milk and solid combination feed to her day.

Should I give my six month-old baby extra water?

Generally breast milk or formula milk is adequate for your baby. There may be occasions when you need to offer her extra water. During very hot weather conditions if after increasing milk supply you still feel she needs more fluid, offer her small amounts of water – 30-60 ml from a bottle, teaspoon or a cup.

CHAPTER 13

Simple feeding sense for your six to 12 month-old

Your little one is now a busy baby and your days are consumed with fitting in sleeps, feeds (which still seem to be non-stop) and some time for play. Your baby will be keen to explore his world and feeding is just one of the areas that excite and inspire him. He will learn from every interaction and meal time in particular will be a time for sensory exploring. His sleep should improve progressively and sleep disturbances during this time will be mostly due to changing nutrition needs and separation anxiety. By following the feeding advice in this chapter you will be able to eliminate hunger as a cause of sleep disruption.

WHAT TO EXPECT IN TERMS OF FEEDING AT THIS STAGE

- **Milk feeds** become secondary to solid food and your baby will drop from four-hourly milk feeds at six months to three feeds by nine months (one on waking in the morning, one after lunch and again at bedtime). By a year, your baby will only need two feeds a day (one on waking and again at bedtime).
- Unless he is ill or not thriving, there is no need for **milk during the night** once your baby is on full solid meals, including protein.
- If you are **bottle feeding**, ensure that his formula is appropriate for his age.
- If you have not yet started your baby on **solid food**, it is essential that you do so as he will be requiring a full **solids** diet now, which includes all the food groups and a good portion of protein three times a day (breakfast, lunch and dinner). (See page 143 for guidelines.)
- Give your baby **control** over his choice of foods and allow him to feed himself from nine months.
- He will enjoy a small finger-food **snack** mid-morning, and mid-afternoon.
- Offer **Rooibos tea** or **water** with every snack and after meals.
- If your baby is eating his solids and is happy, you do not need to worry if his **growth** slows down – he is using up a lot of energy with all the movement.

WHAT YOUR BABY IS UP TO
Development

Your baby is **busy** and active all day and works up an appetite. But being such a busy boy means that he will only sit still and be occupied by feeding for long enough to still his hunger. If he has an interesting activity or can play with his food, he will be more likely to stick around for the entire meal. The **sensory experience** of feeding, from the mushy texture of the food in his hands to the temperature of the food in his mouth, will be a wonderful learning experience for him. This is a good time to **talk** about his food and its sensory qualities.

He will be **sitting** on his own by six to seven months and will be ready for his high-chair. Always supervise your baby whilst in his high-chair. During this phase your baby will start picking up objects with his thumb and forefinger (this is called **pincer grasp**) and move things from one hand to another. This usually happens around nine months, but sometimes a month sooner or later, as each baby is different. This will indicate when your baby is ready to move from mushy foods to self-feeding.

Sleep

Limit your baby's **awake time** to two hours (at six months), increasing steadily to three hours (by a year) between sleeps and plan your care-giving, outings and stimulation within this time. His **day sleeps** will drop from three or four sleeps at six months of age down to two day sleeps by a year. He should sleep for 10 to 12 hours at night. Adequate protein in his diet helps him feel full for longer at night and a wholesome lunch will ensure a longer midday sleep.

FEEDING YOUR SIX TO 12 MONTH-OLD
Milk feeds

Breast-feeding is still beneficial at this stage so, if you can, continue breast-feeding your little one. If he is formula-fed, you need to move him onto a stage two formula. These milks differ in protein quantity and provide extra iron. Your baby does not need more than 500-800 ml of milk per day if on a mixed diet of milk and solids. Once he is on protein, try not to feed him more than once at night as feeding during the night has a significant effect on his appetite for solids. Since solids provide essential nutrients that are no longer found in milk at this age, it is vital that his appetite for solids is not hampered. By the end of the first year, solids will be the predominant provider of nutrition and milk will be secondary but still important.

Your baby will have the following milk feeds:

- Six months: four-hourly which equates to a feed on waking, one at 10 am, one at 2 pm and one at bedtime.
- Nine months: one on waking, one in the afternoon and one at bedtime (he will start to refuse the morning feed as his breakfast quantity increases and a 10 am snack is offered).
- Twelve months: one on waking and one in the evening (as lunch and snacks provide your baby with nutrition, he will drop the afternoon feed).

SENSE-ABLE SECRET
Exceeding 800 ml of milk per day as your baby approaches a year may lead to:
- Insufficient intake of other foods
- Delay in your baby getting used to a variety of tastes and flavours
- Constipation

Solids

Once your baby has more teeth and starts chewing the food better and not pushing it out with his tongue, you know he is ready for a bigger variety of solids. This stage has three major goals: introduce protein, increase variety, offer more texture.

PROTEIN

Protein is important for growth and other functions. There is a range of protein foods to choose from. By ingesting small amounts of protein with each meal and snack time, your baby will remain satisfied for longer and you will know he is receiving enough protein to meet his growing needs. He will get some protein from the milk he continues to drink but the rest will be derived from his solid meals. Aim to offer two tablespoons of protein at each meal. Obviously some meals will have more protein than others and some meals your baby will eat very little altogether. Don't worry – he will make it up in other meals that day.

SENSE-ABLE FEEDING
Most babies will be able to eat all protein foods. If you are concerned about allergies developing or if your baby has a reaction to any particular food, refer to Chapter 6 for guidance.

INTRODUCING PROTEIN

- From six months or just before, depending on when solids were introduced: plain full-cream yogurt, full-cream cottage cheese, soya milk, soya yogurt, chick peas (tinned variety is fine), lentils, broad beans, butter beans, chicken, turkey, ostrich, lamb, beef, low-salt biltong
- From seven to nine months: egg yolk and egg white, fish (hake, tuna, sole, salmon), nuts and seeds (crushed or in paste to avoid choking)
- From nine months: full-cream cow's milk added to cereal, porridge, custard and white sauce.

VARIETY

Variety is important so that by one year your baby is eating a similar diet to the rest of the family. During this stage your baby is developmentally receptive to exploring more foods. If you delay introducing flavours, textures and variety until the toddler years you are more likely to be faced with fussy eating.

WAYS TO INCREASE VARIETY

- Let your baby taste off your plate. A small taste of your gravy or a suck on your meat bone will not harm him and encourages adventurous eating.
- Move from mashed, puréed carrots to softly cooked carrot squares or finely grate raw carrots and let you baby pick it up in his hand.
- Cooking different foods together will also bring different taste combinations, so offer lasagna instead of mince on its own.
- Fruit that was once boiled and puréed, can now be raw and grated or mashed like apple and banana.
- Exposing your baby to lovely kitchen smells and allowing him to handle and play with the foods all add to the feeding experience and increase the exposure to a greater variety of foods.
- By nine months your baby should have been exposed to at least 24 different foods.

WHAT FOODS SHOULD BE INCLUDED?

Orange vegetables	Butternut, hubbard squash, pumpkin, carrot, patty pans, sweet potato, grated beetroot, cooked tomato
Green vegetables	Gem squash, baby marrow, broccoli, spinach, parsnips, cooked onion, garlic, cucumber sticks
Fruit	Pureed, grated raw, mashed raw and juiced. Pears, apples, peaches, pawpaw, melon, banana, prunes, mango, grapes (peeled), litchis (peeled and de-pipped), strawberries, gooseberries, cherries, blueberries
Breakfast starches	Oats porridge, Maltabella, maize porridge, cereal: maize, oats, rice, wheat, mixed grain
Other starches	Basmati rice, quinoa, barley, millet, potato (mash or pieces), pasta shells (small ones), brown bread toast, rye toast
Finger snack foods	Offer these between meals as nutritious fillers. Teething biscuits, rice cakes (yogurt coated or plain or with chickpea paste spread), low-salt biltong, dried mango, toast fingers, dry Oatees, plain dry Rice Crispies, cut up fruit, and raw vegetables like carrot and cucumber strips, berries, Provitas, Flings (a once a week treat)

TEXTURE

It is important to move your baby from smooth and mushy food to **textured** food, finger food and steamed chunky food. At around ten months he will begin to use a spoon, more as a toy, of course, but any interest in feeding utensils is a positive. Keep offering him milk, cereal, yogurt, fruits and veggies, protein and finger foods, but move away from only mashed food and include larger, solid pieces. This is important for the development of the muscles in his mouth.

Baby-led weaning

This concept is growing in popularity. It entails offering your baby (age appropriate) foods that are soft-cooked and cut or mashed into small, easily manageable pieces so he can feed himself. Similar to breast-feeding on cue, baby-led weaning is a method of introducing solid foods that leaves it up to your baby to decide what and how much to eat. While not necessarily a hands-off approach, baby-led weaning does advocate allowing your baby to make his own food choices.

Modified baby-led weaning is a sensible approach for many babies from nine months of age. Instead of moving to lumpy purées, offer your baby soft, solid, whole foods, like blocks of soft, steamed carrot or potato instead of mashed. Lumpy stage three foods may put your baby off eating as he is unsure whether to swallow or chew, while whole foods are much easier to manage and offer a more predictable texture.

Modified baby-led weaning entails having two bowls on offer – one from which you will feed your baby with a spoon, and another with a variety of finger food from which he can choose. In this way you can feed him some of his meal, but also encourage him to feed himself. Observe him as he experiments with the food and if necessary show him how to take the food to his mouth. This places the emphasis on exploring taste, texture, colour and smell as your baby sets his own pace for the meal, choosing which foods to try. This results in less fussy eating and happier meal times.

> **SENSE-ABLE FEEDING**
> In the process of baby-led weaning your baby learns the skill of chewing and squashing the soft chunks of food between his little gums.

Eating is more than just consuming food. The **social** part of eating is also important. Your baby learns most effectively by watching and imitating others. Where appropriate, from about nine months allow your baby to eat the same food at the same time as the rest of the family. Self-feeding contributes to the development of hand-eye coordination and the muscles of your baby's mouth, while encouraging independence. Some babies refuse to eat solids when offered on a spoon, but happily help themselves to finger food.

Meal preparation

Many parents choose to cook, then blend, mash or strain their own baby food. Baby food prepared in this way has several advantages: it is often less expensive, your baby will enjoy food that tastes much better than the jarred variety, and he will learn to eat more varied textures. Jarred baby food often has added sugar, is more expensive and may be less nutritious than home-cooked.

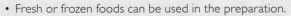

TIPS FOR MAKING YOUR OWN BABY FOOD

- Fresh or frozen foods can be used in the preparation.
- Steaming, baking and boiling are the best cooking methods.
- Microwave cooking is good, especially for vegetables.
- Bananas, pears, strawberries, melons and other soft fruit can be mashed. Be sure to wash all fruit first.
- Home-cooked baby food may be frozen immediately or stored in shallow, covered containers in the refrigerator for one or two days.
- Pour puréed food into ice cube trays and freeze. Once frozen, remove the cubes and store in plastic bags or containers in the freezer for no longer than 2 months. (Be sure to write the date on the plastic bag or container.)

Making food tasty

You can make simple foods really tasty with just a little creative flair and know-how. Fresh herbs like basil and oregano, as well as fresh ginger and garlic, all enhance the flavour of a variety of foods. Look for seasoning agents containing small amounts of organic sea salt mixed with herbs – sprinkle these on meat products before cooking.

Using fruit and lemon juice when cooking your baby's protein dishes will soften the meats and make them easier to liquidize and digest.

Heating baby food

Baby food may be served cold, at room temperature or heated in a saucepan on the stove, or in a dish in the oven or microwave. Stir the food thoroughly to get rid of hot spots and always test by placing some on your wrist to make sure it is not too hot.

Liquids

As your baby eats more solids and milk feeds decrease, he will need additional liquids. Offer him water at room temperature, Rooibos tea without milk or sugar, and flavoured caffeine-free teas – these can be cooled and given as juice.

Avoid fruit juice for as long as possible. Fruit juice has a high sugar and acid content and may cause decay in your baby's developing teeth.

Use this as a general guide for feeds, milk quantities and day sleeps in 24 hours.

Age	Daytime milk feeds	Solid meals	Night feeds	Day sleep
6 months	Breast or formula: 4 feeds a day	Three meals a day with protein introduced	May begin to sleep through or have one night feed between 1 am and 4 am and then morning – 7 am	Two hours between sleeps – three or four sleeps a day
9 months	Breast or formula: 3 feeds a day (150–240 ml)	Three meals a day, all with 1-2 T protein 2 small finger snacks Increase variety	No night feeds; may occasionally still wake for a feed at 4 am	Two to two and a half hours between sleeps
12 months	Milk: 2 feeds, one on waking and one at bed-time (240 ml)	Three meals a day, all with 2 T protein. 2 small finger snacks Modified family meals	No night feeds	Three hours between sleeps during the day; two sleeps a day: a morning nap and a mid-day sleep

Supplements

By this age your baby's **iron stores** have been depleted and must be built up from dietary sources. Breast milk contains little Iron, but it is well absorbed. A breast-fed baby should receive foods with a high iron content – such as animal protein. Formula milk has considerably more added iron but it is not as well absorbed as iron from breast milk. A bottle-fed baby should continue his iron-rich formula until 12 months of age and eat foods with high iron availability. A child with normal iron levels is full of energy and has a healthy glow to his skin. If your child is pale, lacking in energy and eating a diet low in iron-rich foods, consult a healthcare professional as a supplement may be necessary for a period of time. Iron supplementation should only be done under professional guidance. Food rich in iron include infant cereal, spinach, broccoli, peas, egg, beef, baked beans, tuna and chicken.

A HEALTHY MEAL PLAN

During this phase your little one will be learning to eat a balanced diet including a variety of foods which will remain the most important source of his vitamin and mineral intake. If he is slow in weaning or struggling to wean, it is advisable to use a balanced **multivitamin** formulated for babies. If your baby suffers from a chronic disease, fat malabsorption or is on a restricted diet (e.g. he has a food allergy or you follow a vegetarian diet), he may need a multivitamin and mineral supplement.

Your baby will be on a full solids diet. In addition, depending on his appetite, he will be drinking 500-800 ml of milk a day inclusive of milk used in sauces, cereals,

Below is a suggested daily meal plan. Use the lists on page 141 and interchange foods to ensure a good variety of meals and snacks.

MEAL PLAN FOR 6-12 MONTHS

	Food type (choose from lists on page 141)	6-7 months Sample menu	8-9 months Sample menu	10-12 months Sample menu
On waking 6 am	Milk	Milk (180-240 ml)	Milk (180-240 ml)	Milk (180-240 ml)
Breakfast 7-9 am	Starch Protein Fruit	¼-½ cup baby cereal or porridge 1-2 T full-cream plain yogurt Mashed banana	⅓-¾ cup baby cereal or porridge 2 T yogurt Mango pieces	Toast fingers with butter and Bovril 1 boiled egg Pawpaw slices
Snack around 10 am	Finger snack	Milk	Yogurt rice cake Cheese wedges Rooibos tea	Low-salt biltong 2 Provitas baked apple pieces flavoured Rooibos tea juice (recipe p. 166.)
Lunch 12-1 pm	Starch Veggies Protein Fruit	¼-½ cup green veggie mix with sweet potato 1-2 T plain cream cheese mixed into veggies 3 t fruit purée 30 ml water in cup	2 T pasta shells ⅓ cup diced green veggies 4 t Fish bake (recipe p. 163) Sliced pawpaw 30 ml water from a cup	Pita bread triangles 2 teaspoons chickpea mash (recipe p. 162) ¼ avocado, diced ⅓ melon, sliced
Snack around 3 pm	Finger snack	Milk	Milk and teething biscuit	75 ml yogurt Milk(optional) and Oatees
Supper 5-6 pm	Starch Veggies Protein Fruit	¼-½ cup orange veggie mix 2 T chicken and fruit stew (recipe p. 163)	2 T basmati rice ⅓-¾ cup diced steamed carrots, butternut and slices of cucumber 2 T lentil stew (recipe p. 163) Grapes	2 T macaroni with ⅓ cup savoury veggie mince (can be made as a pasta dish) ⅓ cup custard (recipe p. 163) Strawberries
Bedtime	Milk	Milk	Milk	Milk
Night-time	Milk	Small milk feed if required early morning		

HAS MY BABY HAD ENOUGH?

Let your baby take the lead with eating. If you find this hard to do, remember that it is your job to provide him with healthy options, but ultimately he will decide how much he eats:

- Wait for your baby to open his mouth before you put the spoon in.
- Let him touch his food – in the dish or on the spoon.
- Allow him to feed himself with his fingers as soon as he shows an interest.
- Feed him at his own pace. Do not try to make him go slower or faster than he wants to.
- Stop feeding when he shows he has had enough. Do not force him to finish his food. A baby who is full will close his mouth, turn his head away, cover his mouth with his hand, shake his head, or cry if forced to eat more.
- Do not put any food into your baby's mouth without his permission.
- Avoid playing games which trick him into eating.

Weight gain

Your baby's weight gain slows down over this period. Your six month-old will gain around 100 g per week, while your year-old toddler gains as little as 60 g a week. Remember not to look at only one week's weight gain as your baby may gain more one week and much less or even nothing another week. You should not be weighing your baby more than once a month, so watch for a trend on his growth chart. The only time you should be concerned is if there is weight loss or no gain over a month.

YOUR BABY'S HEALTH

Teething

Between six and nine months your baby's first tooth will probably emerge. Teething may cause some disruption in eating for a few days, but the end result will be a tooth, which is getting your baby closer to being an independent eater. Keep perspective and know that teething is nothing to fear.

Health

Sterilising bottles and baby items is pointless now. Everything your baby touches goes into his mouth and these are certainly not all sterile. Go for cleanliness and don't be obsessed about sterilising everything.

Fevers are common at this age. Try to assess how sick your baby is. The most infections by far in this age group are viruses and the immune system will sort the infection out without treatment. If your baby is drinking and sleeping and generally happy, the infection is mild. If the fever is raging, your baby is feeding poorly and battling to breathe, the infection is more serious. Seek medical help. If a fever persists for two or more days with no other worrying symptoms developing, have your baby checked out. It is important to check his urine for a possible infection.

Constipation

If your baby is constipated, increase the amount of water he drinks after a meal and offer diluted prune juice (5 ml prune juice to 30 ml water). Make sure he is getting enough fruit and veggies.

COMMON FEEDING ISSUES

My ten month-old is becoming fussy and even refusing some foods. Should I worry?

It is not uncommon for babies to refuse foods or to become very fussy about food choices around nine months of age. This is just another manifestation of your baby's developing social skills and exerting his independence. Offer him the healthy items you know will be eaten and enjoyed even if you give him the same meal again and again. With every meal, offer a new food item he can hold or explore. Sit down at the table with him and have your own plate of healthy food. A no-fuss approach and a good example will pre-empt or settle down any feeding mayhem.

As he gets used to solids your baby will change his likes and dislikes. What he loved last month, he may no longer want to eat this month. It is important to watch his cues and to use the techniques of baby-led weaning to establish what his ever-changing preferences are. Refusal can be a sign that you need to add variety to the tastes, textures and flavours of his food. Don't be tempted to increase his milk intake as this will just set him back and he will be less likely to eat his solid foods. Rather let him explore new foods with your guidance.

I have a high allergy-risk baby. How do I deal with the introduction of solids now that he's six months old?

It is very important to introduce a wide variety of tastes and textures during the next six months. Protein foods will be a large part of this. Even if your baby has allergies or is a high allergy-risk baby, you must still introduce a variety of proteins. Delaying this past six months will not offer any more protection against allergies; instead, it will put your baby at a higher risk of nutritional deficiency and becoming a fussy eater.

When introducing a new food, watch for signs of allergy, including hives, swelling, wheezing, stuffy nose and itchy, watery eyes, eczema, nausea, vomiting, cramping and diarrhoea. These may occur within a few minutes or a number of days after eating a certain food. Signs of a severe anaphylactic reaction may include hives, swelling, difficulty swallowing or breathing, skin colour changes and dizziness/fainting. Your baby may also pull or scratch at his tongue and talk or cry with a hoarse or squeaky voice. Seek medical attention immediately if these severe symptoms occur.

If your baby experiences any of these symptoms or any other reaction while eating, stop feeding the food you think caused the allergy until you can talk to your baby's doctor or dietician.

If your baby has allergies or is a high allergy-risk baby, follow these guidelines:
- Offer a new protein every 4-6 days – diarize the introduction and any reaction you notice.
- Offer the new foods when you are present and during the earlier part of the day.
- Don't be afraid of food; get guidance and advice so that you can introduce as many foods as possible.
- Avoid the specific allergen if you are already aware of it, e.g. cow's milk protein initially includes all dairy products. You can introduce these foods at an appropriate age under the guidance of your doctor and dietician.

Are there foods I should avoid feeding my nine month-old?

The greater the variety of foods you offer your baby in the months leading up to his first birthday, the better the chances of having a healthy eater who will eat a variety of food, ensuring an adequate nutritional intake.

Once your baby is comfortably on the road to solids you can let him try different tastes and flavours off your plate when you are eating. If you are eating a nutritious meal, don't worry about the very small quantities of salts, sugars and other ingredients your baby will be exposed to.

When it comes to the food that you are cooking specifically for your baby, avoid the following:
- **Salt in the form of sodium chloride** (Table salt or NaCl on packaging): Use a small amount of Himalayan sea salt or organic sea salt mixed with herbs in your cooking. There is no need to add salt to the food on your baby's plate.
- **Sugar**: Sugary foods and drinks can lead to tooth decay when your baby's teeth appear. Sweetened puddings, biscuits, chocolate, sweets and drinks should be avoided as you want to use this time to introduce your baby to healthy food options and natural sweetness in fruits and vegetables.
- **Honey:** Very occasionally honey contains a type of bacteria that can produce toxins in your baby's intestines. Until his immune system is able to cope with this at one year of age, honey should be avoided. Honey is also a sugar and can lead to tooth decay.
- **Whole nuts:** Don't give any *whole nuts*, including peanuts, to children under three owing to the risk of choking. Chopped nuts, seeds, nut pastes and peanut butter should all be introduced as they contain protein, essential fatty acids and are a wonderful form of energy.
- **Low fat, low calorie and high fibre:** It isn't advisable to give any of these foods to babies. They have small tummies and are growing fast. They need food that provides lots of calories and nutrients in a small amount of food, rather than bulky high-fibre foods. High-fibre versions of foods reduce the amount of some minerals that your baby can absorb, like calcium and iron. Fat gives your baby energy and provides some vitamins that are only found in fat. So choose full fat dairy foods.

- Other foods to avoid -
  - Raw and lightly cooked eggs
  - Soft and unpasteurized cheeses
  - Sushi and shellfish
  - Foods containing additives, food colouring or preservatives
  - Highly spiced foods
  - Foods or drinks containing alcohol or caffeine, coffee, tea, cocoa, chocolate
  - Carbonated drinks

My eight month-old happily eats his solids at crèche, but refuses to eat at home. How do I manage this?

If your baby is eating two meals and a snack at crèche or is having a nutritious breakfast at home and a big lunch at school, he may not need or have the appetite for a big supper too. Offer him the food he really likes for supper such as yogurt, cheese and fruit. By following baby-led weaning, you will probably entice your baby to eat a plate of finger food with greater ease than a big bowl of mush.

You may find that he eats better at crèche, where he is eating socially with other children. Add this social element to your meals at home by sitting at the table with your baby and eating with him.

I find mealtimes turning into a circus with my 12 month-old throwing food on the floor. Is he too young to learn about table manners?

Mealtime boundaries can be set from as young as six months and are an important part of your baby's social development. Follow these suggestions:

Boundary	How to introduce
Meal times	From six months, have set meal and snack times each day. This allows your baby to develop an appetite and to expect food at given times. Be flexible and give nutritious snacks with appropriate gaps so the time between meals is not too long for comfort.
Eat sitting down	Give a simple, firm but loving instruction: "Sit down." If your baby keeps standing in his high-chair, remove him for a while and put him back after two minutes.
Eat in a consistent place	This creates a feeding zone which your baby will associate with feeding and where he will be prepared to eat. If your baby is two years or older, consider using a small table and chair as his special place for mealtimes. Do not follow your toddler around with food.

Boundary	How to introduce
Do not throw food on the floor	Teach your baby a signal for finished: clap hands together and open them up. If your baby is over a year of age, give a firm instruction: "No, we don't throw food."
Say please and thank you	Repeat 'please' and 'thank you' *every time* your baby indicates he wants something ('please') or receives something ('thank you'/'ta'). If your baby is not speaking yet, teach hand signals: · Please: flat hand rubbing his chest · Thank you: four fingertips to lips and then towards you.

All done

Thank you

CHAPTER 14

Simple feeding sense for your toddler

The toddler years are a time of laughs and fun. Your baby's personality emerges and she loves to play. Although your life will never be the same as before her birth, you are settling down as you are not as bound by sleep and feed times as before – your baby is simply much more flexible. But just when you get a handle on feeding this little person, she develops a very strong will and discovers that meal times are the perfect arena to assert her new-found independence and autonomy. It has been said that toddlers exist on fresh air and love!

WHAT TO EXPECT IN TERMS OF FEEDING AT THIS STAGE

- **Milk feeds** are secondary to all other forms of food and essentially if your toddler still has a milk bottle before bed, it is more for comfort than because she needs it nutritionally.
- No toddler needs milk feeds during the **night** – it does more harm than good.
- Most toddlers will not need to be on a formula milk of any kind, **full-fat cow's milk** is fine at this stage.
- Your toddler should be on a **fully solid** diet, which should be extensive and varied.
- Three meals of **finger foods** and two **snacks** are the order of the day and your toddler will prefer whole food to mashed food.
- Feeding toddlers can be **challenging**. They are often picky eaters, are hesitant to try new foods, and in general, don't seem to eat very much.

WHAT YOUR TODDLER IS UP TO
Development
Your **busy** toddler may not always have time to eat. If she is heavily engrossed in a task in the garden or playing with her toys, she will resist the idea of being taken away to eat.

The developmental task of the toddler years is to develop **autonomy**. Your toddler will be flexing her muscles in every area, from dressing to bedtime to meals. You need to take a positive attitude towards her emerging independence and give her the opportunity to 'control' meal times, within boundaries (see page 148). You can do this by giving a choice between two foods, both of which you are happy with – for example a choice of porridge or bacon and eggs for breakfast; a choice of eating in her high-chair or at the toddler table in the garden (as long as she is sitting for meals it doesn't matter where she is). These are two simple ideas of acceptable choices for your toddler to make herself.

It is very important to understand your role and your toddler's role. **Your responsibility** is threefold:

1. To provide your little one with a **variety** of healthy foods, some she enjoys and some that are new and challenging, at each meal.
2. To choose the **time** of feeding – feeding your toddler at a similar time every day will allow her body to expect food at those times. This allows her to develop an appetite. Making available frequent, evenly spaced opportunities to eat will also assist this process.
3. Determine **where** the food will be served: in a high-chair, at the big table, at a small table and chair, on a picnic blanket, etc.

Your **toddler's responsibility** when all the above is in place is to decide **how much** she will eat. Understanding and defining these areas takes most of the battle out of eating. It is not a power struggle, rather you and your toddler embarking on an eating journey together.

Your toddler's **dexterity** will continue to be developed at meal times. She will explore self-feeding, first with fingers and then with utensils. Give her many opportunities to practise these skills, but lend a hand when frustrations arise. As skills develop, step back and let your toddler take over.

Sleep
Your toddler needs her **day sleep** until she is a little older. Some toddlers drop the midday sleep as early as two and a half years old and others love a nap right up to five years of age. Follow your toddler's lead. She should be sleeping 11 to 12 hours at night and **night wakings** are typically due to health issues and toddler behaviour as opposed to poor nutrition. If your toddler's diet is very limited, an iron supplement and plant protein in the form of dissolvable barley green can make a difference to her sleep.

FEEDING YOUR TODDLER
Milk and other liquids
Milk is no longer needed on its own. It can be made available in other forms such as yogurt, cheese and custards or can be offered in tea or in cereals. From one year old most babies can switch from formula to full-fat cow's milk. After two years of age, move your toddler onto low-fat cow's milk. Only one milk feed a day is needed in the toddler years, usually in a bottle or cup at night before bed.

Your toddler should only drink water, Rooibos tea or very diluted fruit juice (mixed four parts water to one part pure fruit juice). The aim is to encourage water drinking at this age. Keep a water bottle filled and on offer at all times for when your toddler is thirsty. Keep juice as a drink only at snack time.

Meal times

At this age your toddler is moving from the eating habits she had as a baby towards a diet more like your own. You should prepare balanced meals and healthy snacks for her. Well-balanced choices, especially during snack time, will help you to compensate for smaller portions being eaten at meal time. Your toddler's eating and sleeping routine is likely to resemble this:

Age	Daytime milk feeds	Solid meals	Night feeds	Day sleep
1–2 years	Milk: One milk feed in the evening before bed and a cup of tea on waking (240 ml per feed)	Three meals a day, each with 2 T protein 2 small finger snacks Modified family meals	No night feeds	Two sleeps; the morning nap will fall away shortly after one year of age
2–3 years	Milk in tea and dairy in meals	Family meals and two snacks	No night feeds	One sleep at midday

Serving sizes

Feeding your toddler becomes less complicated and frustrating if you realize how small a serving size for a toddler really is. Your toddler's tummy is only the size of her fist, so as little as three tablespoons of a varied meal may be enough for her. Do offer more than this but don't be disappointed if that is all she eats. Give her a number of small meals every day and do not expect her to eat large quantities at three main meals like adults. Also be sure to serve foods that are packed with the nutrients she needs to grow healthy and strong. Limit sweets and empty calorie foods such as chips and cakes.

You may notice as the day progresses that your toddler becomes less and less hungry. Rest assured, it is common for toddlers to eat well at breakfast, eat okay at lunch and come dinner time eat either tiny bites or leave behind a virtually full plate.

Many of the eating problems experienced during the first three years of life are due to unrealistic expectations. So do try and keep this in mind when planning and preparing food for your toddler. Both you and your toddler will experience less stress and meals will be pleasant, happy times if you offer her portions suitable for her age and let her eat five or six small meals a day.

Toddler preferences

Toddlers develop strong preferences for certain foods – your little one may eat only fruit one day, and vegetables the next. Since erratic eating habits are as normal as toddler mood swings, expect your toddler to eat well one day and practically nothing the next. Aim for a nutritionally balanced week, not a balanced day.

A HEALTHY MEAL PLAN FOR TODDLERS

Meals	Times	Food ideas	Approximate amounts
Morning milk	6 am	Full-cream cow's milk in tea	150 ml
Breakfast	8 am	Cereal, dry Milk Yogurt Fruit	2-3 T 50 – 100 ml 2 T ¼ apple, sliced
Snack	10 am	Fruit (for dipping): Peanut butter dip Mini yogurt-coated rice cake Diluted juice/ Rooibos tea	¼ peach ¼ banana 1 t 1 150-200 ml
Lunch	1 pm	Toddler smorgasbord (recipe page 166) Water	
Snack	3 pm	Yogurt fruit smoothie or fruit ice lolly	75-150 ml
Supper	5:30 pm	Fishcakes Pasta shells Corn pieces Butternut squares Water	½ – 1 ¼ cup 1 T 3 mini dice size
Bedtime milk	7 pm	Bottle/Cup full-cream cow's milk	240 ml

Getting your toddler to eat

This meal plan may look great in theory but in practice getting your toddler to eat may be a challenge. To assist you along the way here are some tips to get your toddler eating:

OFFER A NIBBLE TRAY

Toddlers like to graze their way through a variety of foods, so offer your little one a customized smorgasbord. Use an ice-cube tray, a muffin tin, or a compartmentalized dish, and put bite-size portions of colourful and nutritious food in each section. Call these finger foods playful names that a two-year-old can appreciate (see page 166).

DIP IT

Young children think that immersing foods in a tasty dip is pure fun (and delightfully messy). Dips serve equally well as spreads on apple or pear slices, red pepper strips, rice cakes, toast, or other nutritious platforms. Ideas of nice dips:
- cottage cheese
- mashed fruit purée
- mashed avocado
- peanut butter, thinly spread
- puréed vegetables
- yogurt, plain or sweetened with fruit pulp

SPREAD IT

Toddlers like spreading, or more accurately, smearing. Show your little one how to use a table knife to spread cheese, peanut butter and fruit concentrate onto crackers, toast or rice cakes.

DRINK IT

If your youngster would rather drink than eat, don't despair. Make a smoothie together.

CUT IT UP

How much a child will eat often depends on how you cut it. Cut sandwiches, pancakes, waffles and pizza into various shapes using cookie cutters.

PACKAGE IT

Appearance is important. For something new and different, why not use your baby's own toy plates for dishing out a snack?

RAISING A VEGGIE LOVER

Try to use fresh vegetables and don't overcook them. Steam veggies until they are tender but still sweet and crispy. This way your toddler experiences veggies as tasty, not mushy, food.
- Add grated or diced vegetables to rice, cottage cheese, cream cheese, guacamole, or even macaroni and cheese.
- Make baby marrow pancakes and carrot muffins.
- Use vegetables as finger foods and dip them into a favourite sauce or dip.
- Use a small cookie cutter to cut the vegetables into interesting shapes.
- Make veggie art – create colourful faces with olive-slice eyes, tomato ears, mushroom noses, bell-pepper moustaches, and any playful features you can imagine.
- Plant a garden with your child. Let her help care for the plants, harvest the ripe vegetables, and wash and prepare them. She will probably be much more interested in eating what she has helped to grow.

USE SIT-STILL STRATEGIES

One reason why toddlers don't like to sit still at the family table is that their feet dangle. Try sitting on a bar stool while eating. You naturally begin to squirm and want to get up and move around. Your toddler is more likely to sit and eat longer at a child-size table and chair where her feet touch the ground.

LET THEM COOK

Children are more likely to eat their own creations, so, when appropriate, let your toddler help prepare the food.

HAS MY TODDLER HAD ENOUGH?

In planning your toddler's diet, it helps to bear in mind she needs a lot less to eat than you think. Remember, she isn't growing as fast as during her first year of life and so has lower energy needs and a smaller appetite. If your toddler is active, healthy, and growing and developing normally, she is most likely getting plenty to eat. Don't worry if your toddler:

- Doesn't seem to eat a lot. As long as she is gaining weight and is active and healthy, she is getting enough calories.
- Only eats a few kinds of food each day, such as peanut butter sandwiches, hot dogs, or chicken and noodles, only fruit or only vegetables.
- Won't try any new foods. You can keep trying to introduce new foods by putting a very small amount (½-1 tablespoon) on her plate. Don't force her to try or finish it. Many children won't try a new food until they have been exposed to it ten or more times.
- Doesn't eat a balanced diet each day. Most toddlers don't. As long as her diet seems balanced over a week or two, she is likely getting enough variety. If she really isn't, talk to your paediatrician about the need for a vitamin supplement.
- Doesn't finish everything on her plate. The idea that children should sit at the table until they 'clean' their plate is outdated. Instead, teach your toddler to recognize when she is full and then stop eating. If she isn't finishing what you offer, offer smaller portions.
- Doesn't eat what you prepare for her. Try to avoid making elaborate meals for your toddler or offering foods with a lot of spices or sauces. Instead, keep things simple. While you shouldn't have to prepare a separate meal for your toddler every day, don't be surprised if she doesn't want to eat 'adult' foods.

Weight gain

Your toddler will gain approximately 250 g per month between a year and two years of age. Thereafter she will gain around 180 g per month. You will probably no longer weigh her much and will judge whether she is thriving based on her energy levels and health.

If your toddler is very skinny and low in energy and regularly ill, seek the advice of a dietician who will assist you in supplementing her diet.

You should be a little concerned if your child is overweight, even at this age. However, instead of restricting calories, you may just want to provide a healthy diet and encourage regular physical activity. Be sure to watch your serving and portion sizes (offer toddler size portions) and don't offer too much milk, juice, or high calorie snacks.

YOUR TODDLER'S HEALTH
Supplements

There is no need to start additional vitamins as long as your toddler has a good appetite and enjoys a full diet. If she is a very fussy eater and eats a limited choice, additional vitamins and minerals will be necessary. If she does not eat a lot of meat products, she will need additional iron and if she won't eat fruit and vegetables, she should have a vitamin supplement. If your toddler is ill and does not eat for a prolonged period, she should have supplements in the form of shakes. These shakes are provided in powder form that you mix with water or milk and provide a meal in a cup. Some of the products are ready to drink. Ask your doctor or dietician about these supplements.

Fussy eating

Children at crèche or day care often eat better at their day-time venue than at home. They often have breakfast at crèche and then a mid-morning snack followed by lunch and then a snack in the afternoon. With this much food it is no surprise that they are not hungry at supper. In this situation offer your toddler a small, nutritious snack for supper. Likewise, your toddler may not eat well on weekends and this is just because the eating at crèche is a social occasion with her friends and everyone eats together. Try to make sure you sit down to meals together because your toddler will learn from the example you set. If you don't eat vegetables then it is unlikely that your child will want to eat vegetables; if you don't sit down to a meal at a table then your child won't either.

Teething

Teething continues and the last of your baby's 20 teeth appears at around 30 months. This may affect her appetite temporarily but is no reason for concern. Offer teething biscuits and low-fat biltong.

Childhood illnesses

Most of the childhood illnesses occur during the toddler years, and a sick toddler is likely to eat poorly if at all. You need not be too concerned about this as your toddler would have been vaccinated against the serious illnesses. Bear in mind that a toddler going to crèche or play group is more likely to have frequent coughs and colds, as well as gastroenteritis and ear infections. Do not force your child to eat if she is not feeling well, but ensure that she has enough fluids.

COMMON FEEDING ISSUES
What can I do about my picky eater?

Your toddler's eating patterns develop from earliest infancy and lay the foundation for later eating habits. Many factors shape eating patterns, including your family's attitude to food, the foods your baby is exposed to in the first year, the social context of meal times and your baby's genes and health. If your toddler is a very picky eater, you could follow these strategies:

- Expose her repeatedly to new foods. It is normal for a child to reject a food at first, but acceptance can be encouraged by offering it repeatedly in a supportive way. Your baby may need to see, touch and explore the food up to ten times before she will try it.
- Eat together with your picky eater to add a social element to meal times.
- If your toddler associates an illness with a specific food, she may avoid that specific food. Offering a new food with similar properties to the rejected food may assist the road to acceptance.
- Set appropriate boundaries and routines around meal and snack times. Even if your child doesn't eat all the food on offer, the important thing is that a variety of healthy food was offered in a relaxed, calm environment at a set place and time.
- Be sensitive to your child's pace and readiness to try a new food. Avoid comparing your toddler with the toddler next door who eats everything and more!

My toddler drinks a litre of milk a day and has two night feeds. She is a fussy eater. What can I do?

You need to be concerned if your toddler is drinking excessive amounts of liquid to the detriment of her appetite for solids. If she has this much milk, she will not get adequate protein, and lack important vitamins and minerals present in solid food.

Your toddler needs to be hungry to eat more solid and age-appropriate foods. She really only needs one bottle of 240 ml in a 24-hour period and the rest of her dairy should be milk in tea and dairy in solid meals. She also only needs water after meals and a small cup of diluted juice with each snack. Any more fluids than this will affect her appetite. Reduce the milk and juice she has and stick to these boundaries. You may be concerned about her feeling hungry for a day or two but she will slowly look for other ways to nourish her needy body. It is helpful to get some professional support to reassure you when you have to cope with the resulting tantrums and hunger strikes. Keeping a food diary is very helpful and will assist both you and the health professional advising you to determine if there are any nutrient gaps and monitor the risk of deficiencies.

Be consistent and resolved and employ the other bits of advice listed in this chapter and you should be well on your way to raising a child with healthy eating habits.

My doctor says my toddler is not growing properly and she is a fussy eater. What should I do?

It is one thing to have a fussy eater, who is a healthy, happy and energetic toddler. But when faced with a toddler who is not only fussy, but also growing poorly, it is understandably a big concern for you. Along with all the strategies we have given you in this chapter and helping your fussy eater to eat, you also need to improve her nutritional status while you implement the strategies and can't wait until she is no longer fussy to ensure she is getting an adequate intake.

ADD ENERGY BOOSTERS TO YOUR TODDLER'S MEAL:

- Powdered milk – full-cream powdered cow's or soya milk: Add to mince, mashed potatoes and milkshakes as well as yogurt and cooked cereals.
- Cheese: Full-fat white cheese: Add grated cheese or cheese sauce to mashed potatoes, scrambled eggs or sprinkle on bread.
- Cooked egg yolk: Can be added to all kinds of food, such as white sauce.
- Peanut butter: Makes a great spread on toast, muffins and waffles. Peanut butter also tastes great in milkshakes, cookies and puddings.
- Commercial calorie drinks: A variety of commercial high-protein and energy drinks are available, for example Paediasure and Nutren Junior. They come in different flavours, so try different ones to find your child's favourite.
- A good *multivitamin and mineral supplement* will also be important for your toddler at this stage.

Appendix A

GROWTH CHARTS

Growth charts are useful to track the weight gain and growth of your baby and toddler, but it is very important to realize that there is a wide variation in the height and weight of babies and children. They show the **international average** for weight and height for each age group according to their gender. The curved pattern lines show you where your baby is compared with others. If your baby is above the bold line, he is bigger compared with other babies of the same age and gender.

While you must not be too concerned about your baby's growth chart, reasons to see your doctor include:

- If your baby's weight or height curve changes from the pattern it has been following
- If your baby doesn't grow taller at the same rate at which he is gaining weight
- If your baby doesn't gain sufficient weight for his height·
- If one of the parameters is out of proportion. For example if the head and the length are on the 97th percentile and the weight is on the 3rd percentile
- Any sudden increase or decrease in any growth measurement.

Using a growth chart

Aside from knowing that all babies grow differently, it is important to realize that the average curve for boys differ from that of girls, and that a breast-fed baby's curve will differ from that of a bottle-fed baby.

Your healthcare professional will measure your baby's weight, height and head circumference and plot these on your baby's chart. If these measurements are in proportion and your baby is growing well, you can rest assured. This means that even if your baby is underweight but growing, there is no need for concern if she is also short and has a smallish head. However, if your baby is overweight and short, or is of normal weight and length but has a small head, your doctor may want to monitor her closely.

The growth chart provides essential information to assess the general health of your baby and the measurements should be recorded at every visit to the clinic or the doctor. This enables you to track your baby's growth relative to the general population but also relative to himself. If your baby is born at 3,5 kg (50th percentile for birth) and continues to grow along the 50th percentile, you know that he is growing well. The same applies to the head circumference and the length. If your baby starts on the 10th percentile, it is not a problem as long as the growth follows on or close to the 10th percentile throughout his life. When the growth lines start to cross over percentiles suggesting a rapid drop or a rapid rise in weight or height or head size, it may be an indication of a problem. Premature babies and babies born small for gestational age may catch up their growth and cross percentile lines in a positive direction. This is acceptable, but must be monitored to ensure that the baby is not growing too quickly.

Premature babies have growth charts specifically designed for premature babies and their growth must be strictly monitored – initially on a daily basis to ensure that they are growing adequately, and then twice a week until they are discharged from hospital. By the age of one a premature baby should weigh and be the size that he would have been at that age had he not been born prematurely. Once a premature baby has reached an age equivalent to a full-term pregnancy he is plotted on a standard growth chart.

Children with recognized syndromes must be plotted on the relevant graphs. For example children with achondroplasia (little people or dwarfs) should be plotted on graphs specific to them.

Appendix B

RECIPES

It is a good idea to make more home-cooked food than you need and freeze the excess, especially when you are weaning. Most purées freeze brilliantly except those made with banana or avocado.

For freezing you need some clean ice-cube trays with lids. As your baby gets older, slightly larger sealed containers that can hold about 180-250 ml are recommended.

TO FREEZE AND DEFROST:
- Cool food down quickly
- Always label and date the food
- Ideally defrost food in the refrigerator overnight, although for small cubes of purée this is not necessary – just reheat them in a bowl over a saucepan of boiling water.
- Make sure food is thoroughly reheated
- Never refreeze
- Freeze food containing dairy for up to six weeks
- Freeze fruit and vegetables for up to eight weeks
- Freeze food containing meat, chicken and fish for up to three months.

F = SUITABLE FOR FREEZING

4 – 6 MONTHS

Your four to six month-old may initially eat 3 t (teaspoons). As your baby gets older, offer servings of up to 10 t and follow her lead. A serving may vary between 3 t and 10 t depending on her appetite.

FIRST VEGGIE MIX

- 4 medium gem squash
- 3 medium sweet potatoes, red
- 8 medium baby marrows

1. Cook the gem quash in boiling water. Scoop out the pips, remove the pulp and liquidize. Strain through a sieve and set aside.
2. Peel and steam the sweet potato.
3. Steam the baby marrows until soft.
4. Liquidize the sweet potato and baby marrow together. Strain through a sieve and mix with gem squash.

Makes 50-80 servings

ORANGE VEGGIE MIX

- 1 medium hubbard squash, diced (by your local fruit and veg shop)
- 2 medium parsnips, peeled and diced
- 6 medium carrots, peeled and diced

1. Steam or bake the diced veggies, cool and liquidize them all together until smooth.

Makes 30-50 servings

PURÉED APPLE OR PEAR

Boil, steam or microwave a medium apple or pear until tender; drain over small bowl, reserving 1 T cooking liquid. Blend or process fruit with cooking liquid or boiled water until smooth.

Makes 5-10 servings

APRICOT PURÉE WITH BLENDED RICE CEREAL

- 100 g dried apricots
- 2 T blended cereal
- 1½ C water
- ⅓ C formula or breast milk, warmed

1. Combine apricots and water in small saucepan; simmer, covered, about 20 minutes or until apricots are tender.
2. Blend apricots and cooking liquid until smooth.
3. Mix rice cereal in small bowl with breast milk or formula; serve topped with 1 T apricot purée.

Makes 15-25 servings

BEETROOT AND CARROT PURÉE

- 1 fresh medium beetroot, peeled, topped and tailed
- 2 medium carrots, peeled and diced

1. Cook beetroot in boiling water until tender (about 30 minutes). Drain and leave to cool.
3. Steam the peeled and diced carrots until tender.
4. Blend together and liquidize.

Makes 15 servings

LIQUIDIZED/STRAINED OATS

Soak 2 T raw oats in 4 T water, cook until runny. Cool slightly, then liquidize.

Makes 4-6 servings

Your six to 12 month-old's appetite will vary between meals and each day. Offer your baby 6 t. She will eat between 6 and 12 t at a meal.

CHICKPEA MASH

- I tin (410 g) organic chickpeas, drained
- I T lemon juice

1. Remove the chickpea skins.
2. Place in a blender and add lemon juice while blending.
3. Use as a spread on pita, rice cakes, bread or mix into your baby's food.

Makes 15 servings

MASHED POTATOES, GEM SQUASH AND CHICKEN

- ½ chicken breast fillet, diced
- 2 peeled, cooked potatoes
- I large cooked gem squash

1. Place diced chicken in a wire sieve (covered) and steam over a saucepan of boiling water for approximately 10 minutes.
2. Remove gem squash pips, then scoop out the flesh.
3. Liquidize the chicken and vegetables together, adding some of the liquid over which the chicken was steamed.

Makes 3 servings

SCRAMBLED VEGGIE EGGS

For convenience, use hand cut vegetables (carrots, patty pans, green beans and baby marrows). You could also add peas, finely diced cabbage and similar vegetables. Dice the vegetables into smaller pieces.

- ¼ C mixed vegetables
- ¼ C expressed breast milk or formula
- I egg
- ½ t butter or margarine

1. Steam the vegetables until cooked (approximately 5 minutes).
2. Lightly beat egg and milk.
3. Add the veggies to the egg mixture.
4. Melt butter in a frying pan, add egg mix and stir in pan until all the egg is cooked through.

Makes 1-2 servings

LENTIL STEW

- 100 g lentils, raw
- 2 medium carrots
- ½ small butternut/pumpkin
- 50 g brown rice, raw
- 1 medium sweet potato

1. Cook the lentils and rice until soft according to directions on the bag.
2. Steam carrots, sweet potato and butternut, liquidize to a moderately smooth consistency.
3. Add the lentils and rice and serve

Makes 5 servings

CHICKEN AND FRUIT STEW

- 1 medium peach, diced
- 2 medium carrots, diced
- 1 tin (200 g) tomato and onion mix
- 200 ml water
- 1 medium apple, sliced
- 250 g raw chicken, finely chopped
- Mixed herbs

1. Steam fruit and vegetables until soft and tender.
2. Bake the chicken in the tomato and onion mix.
3. Add fruit and veggies to chicken in tomato and liquidize until the texture is right for your baby.

Makes 5 servings

FISH BAKE IN BULK

- 1 kg fresh hake
- 600 g cooked peas
- 5 cooked potatoes, mashed
- 1 large butternut, cooked and mashed
- 2 T milk

1. Steam the fish for 20 minutes, flake and mix with the mashed butternut, peas and milk.
2. Spoon equal portions of fish and vegetable mixture into 14 individual small containers.
3. Top each serving with mashed potato. Freeze at this stage.
4. Reheat from frozen in the microwave or in the oven (covered) at 200°C for about 20 minutes.

Makes 14 servings

BANANA CUSTARD

- 1 small banana
- 1 egg yolk
- 2 t expressed breast milk, formula or milk

1. Mash banana, add egg yolk and milk.
2. Pour into a small, greased ovenproof dish (180 ml) and stand in a Bain Marie and bake at 120°C for about 20 minutes until set.

Makes 1 serving

THICK VEGGIE AND CHICKEN SOUP

- 1 C finely diced, sliced or grated: carrots, beans, tomatoes, spinach, potato, corn, peas and broccoli
- 2 C water
- 1 T msg-free chicken-stock powder
- ½ C chicken breast fillet, finely diced

1. Place vegetables in a saucepan, add water, stock powder and diced chicken.
2. Bring to the boil, boil fast until tender and allow to simmer for a further 40 minutes on low heat.
3. Purée the soup before serving (texture depending on your baby's age).

Makes 3 servings

TODDLER

Follow your toddlers cues on food quantities. Remember, your responsibility is to offer the food. She will eat until she is no longer hungry.

MINI VEGGIE BURGERS

- 1 tin (410 g) red lentils (drained)
- Msg free veggie seasoning
- 1 tin (410 g) chickpeas
- 2 medium grated baby marrows
- 2 T lemon juice
- 1 t salt
- 1 C oats
- 5 ml olive oil
- 2 medium onions
- 1 egg
- 2 medium grated carrots
- 2 t crushed garlic
- 2 T chopped coriander
- 1 C stale breadcrumbs
- plain flour for dusting and egg for coating

1. Fry the onions with the veggie seasoning and garlic until golden brown.
2. In a large bowl, place chickpeas, ½ lentils, egg, coriander, grated carrots, grated marrow and cooked onions and blend in a food processor until chickpeas are broken down.
3. Add the remaining lentils, oats and breadcrumbs. If the mixture is too wet, add more oats. Mix well.
4. Shape portions into small rounds (get your toddler to help). Toss in egg and then breadcrumbs. Place on a tray.
5. Fry for about 4 minutes until golden brown.
6. Serve in a roll or in mini pitas with tomato sauce or plain yoghurt with mint.

Makes 8 veggie burgers

CHEESE AND BABY MARROW MUFFINS (F)

Toddlers love these and they make a great snack.

- 300 g self-raising flour
- 75 g grated cheese
- 1 C plain yogurt
- 3 eggs
- ½ t mustard (optional)
- black pepper (optional)

- 3 T baking powder
- 1 large baby marrow
- 3 T oil
- 3 T milk
- a few basil leaves (optional)
- paper muffin cases

1. Preheat oven to 220°C.
2. Place flour, baking powder and cheese in a mixing bowl.
3. Grate in baby marrow, add yoghurt, oil, eggs, milk and optional seasoning.
4. Lightly mix with a fork until just combined.
5. Spoon in to paper muffin cases, two-thirds full.
6. Add a little grated cheese on top and bake for 15 mins until golden.

Makes 12 muffins

FISH CAKES (F)

Serve with fettucini or fusilli noodles and steamed peas for a balanced meal.

- 1 kg fresh hake, steamed until tender
- 4 slices whole-wheat bread (crusts removed)
- 1 beaten egg
- 2 T olive oil

- 2 C cooked, mashed pumpkin
- 1 C milk
- 2 T finely chopped fresh or dried herbs

1. Flake the fish and mix with the pumpkin.
2. Break the bread into chunks and soak in the milk for approximately 10 minutes.
3. Remove the chunks of bread from the milk and mix with the fish and pumpkin mixture.
4. Add the beaten egg and herbs and mix well.
5. Shape into 28 small fish cakes.
6. Heat the olive oil in an ovenproof dish at 180°C.
7. Place the fish cakes in the dish and cover.
8. Bake for 20 minutes.

Makes 28 fish cakes

SUMMER FRUIT KEBABS

- ¼ C Oatees
- 3 grapes
- ½ banana
- 1 kebab stick

- ½ pear
- ½ slice pineapple
- 2 marshmallows
- ¼ C low-fat yogurt

1. Cut the fruit into squares.
2. Thread fruit squares, marshmallows and Oatees onto the kebab stick.
3. Pour some yogurt in a bowl for dipping.

Makes 1

TODDLER'S SMORGASBORD

Use an ice-cube tray, a muffin tin, or a compartmentalized dish, and place bite-size portions of colourful and nutritious foods in each section. Call these finger foods playful names that a two-year-old can appreciate, such as:

- apple moons (thinly sliced)
- banana wheels
- carrot swords (cooked and thinly sliced)
- egg canoes (hard-boiled egg wedges)
- avo boats (a quarter of an avocado)
- broccoli trees (steamed broccoli florets)
- cheese building blocks
- Oatees – little O's

ICED TEA

- 4 flavoured Rooibos tea bags
- 250 ml clear, pure fruit juice
- 1 litre boiling water
- 1 T lemon juice

1. Boil water and pour over tea bags.
2. Add 250 ml fruit juice and lemon juice.
3. Cool in fridge.

Makes 10 servings – it will keep well in the fridge

RECIPES FOR ALLERGIES

BANANA MUFFINS   F

Egg, dairy, soya and nut free

- 3 ripe bananas (overripe make the best muffins)
- 1 C sugar
- 1 C raisins/currants (optional)
- a sprinkle of coconut (optional)
- 2 C flour
- ¼ C oil
- 1 t bicarb of soda
- a handful of oatmeal (optional)
- 1 t salt

1. Pre-heat over to 180°C.
2. Mash bananas, add oil and sugar and mix well. Add any or all optional ingredients if desired.
4. Sift flour, salt and bicarb of soda together and add to banana mixture.
5. Mix until flour is blended (do not beat).
6. Spoon into muffin pans and bake until a toothpick comes out clean.

Makes 12 muffins

CHERRY AND APPLE QUINOA

Dairy, soya, egg, wheat and nut free

This is great any time of day, especially for breakfast

- 25 g quinoa
- 1 apple, peeled, cored and chopped
- Clear honey

- 25 g cherries
- 200 ml water
- Dairy-free milk or cream substitute to serve

1. Rinse the quinoa thoroughly in a sieve, tip into a non-stick saucepan and add the cherries, apples and water.
2. Bring to the boil, reduce the heat and simmer gently for about 20 minutes until the grains are soft and moist, with most of the liquid absorbed.
3. Sweeten to taste with honey. Serve in a bowl with a little milk or cream substitute.

Makes 1 serving

CREAMY TOMATO SOUP

Dairy, soya, wheat, egg and nut free

- 1 small onion, chopped
- 1 can (410 g) of tomatoes
- 30 ml tomato purée (paste)
- 25 ml castor sugar (superfine)
- 150 ml dairy-free milk

- 2 T dairy-free margarine
- 300 ml vegetable stock, made with one dairy-free/gluten-free stock cube
- 15 ml arrowroot (health shops/supermarkets)
- Salt and freshly ground black pepper

1. Sauté the onion in the margarine for 1 minute, stirring occasionally. Reduce the heat to low, cover and sweat the onion for 5 minutes until softened but not browned.
2. Add the tomatoes and break up with a wooden spoon. Stir in the stock, tomato purée and sugar. Bring to the boil, reduce the heat, part-cover and simmer gently for 15 minutes.
3. Blend thoroughly in an electric blender.
4. Blend the arrowroot with the milk in the saucepan. Pour the soup back in the saucepan and bring to the boil, stirring, until thickened. Do not continue to boil. Season to taste and serve.

Makes 4 servings

CORN FRITTERS

Dairy, soya, gluten, wheat and egg free.

- ⅓ C rice flour
- A good pinch of salt
- 7 T water
- Sunflower oil, for cooking

- ⅓ C cornflour (cornstarch)
- 1 T gluten-free baking powder
- 1 tin (200 g) of sweetcorn, drained

1. Mix the flours with the salt and baking powder.
2. Stir in the water to form a thick, creamy batter.
3. Stir in the sweetcorn.
4. Pour enough oil into a frying pan to cover the base and heat. Drop in spoonfuls of the batter. Fry until golden underneath. Turn over and cook until crisp. Drain on kitchen paper. Serve warm.

Makes 12 corn fritters

HOMEMADE BREAD

Dairy, wheat, egg, soya and nut free.

Grate the skin of the apple as well as the flesh, because the pectin, which helps the bread to rise, is just under it.

- A little oil, for greasing
- 1 sachet of easy-blend dried yeast
- 1 eating (dessert) apple
- 1 C lukewarm water

- 2 C Orgran flour mix plus a little for dusting
- ½ t salt
- 1 T sunflower oil

1. Preheat the oven to 200°C.
2. Grease a 450 g loaf tin and dust with a little of the flour.
3. Put all the ingredients except the water in a large mixing bowl and mix well. Add the water and beat until the mixture forms a thick batter.
4. Pour into the prepared tin. Place in a warm place for 15 minutes and leave to rise until the dough almost reaches the top of the tin.
5. Stand the tin in a roasting tin containing about 2,5 cm of boiling water. Bake towards the top the oven for 1 hour.
6. Turn out of the tin, place upside-down on the oven shelf and bake for a further 15 minutes to crisp the crust. Cool on a wire rack.

Makes 1 small loaf

Appendix C

ALLERGY REPLACEMENT FOODS

Milk	
Allergy to cow's milk protein occurs in about 2% of children under the age of three years and 85% of these children will outgrow the allergy by 3 years of age.	
Symptoms • Itching and swelling of the lips • Tummy cramps, nausea, vomiting • Asthma • Inflammation of the intestines causing poor absorption, nausea, diarrhoea and sometimes anaphylaxis.	• Eczema • Hay fever
Avoid	**Replacement foods**
• Chocolate, Ice cream • Yoghurt • Custard • Butter, margarine	• Dairy-free ice cream and chocolate • Soya yogurt (if not allergic to soya) • Soya or rice milk custard • Cardin or dairy-free margarine
Read the labels Whey, casein, cream, milk solids, any ingredient that starts with *lacto-*	**Labels** Rice milk, oat milk powder, soya milk if no soya allergy present

Wheat	
It is not uncommon for children to react adversely to wheat but to test negative in an allergy wheat test. True wheat allergy is very uncommon.	
Symptoms • Skin – hives, eczema • Asthma	• Tummy – cramps, nausea, vomiting • Hay fever
Avoid	**Replacement foods**
• Wheat, bran, pasta, pies, pastries, couscous, confectionery, pizza, cakes, bread (white and brown), biscuits, tarts, yeast • Breakfast cereals: Weetbix, muesli, Tasti Wheat, semolina, Pro Nutro	• Rice, quinoa, millet, sago, barley, amaranth, buckwheat, spelt ,oats, gluten-free products, soya, rye, arrowroot, corn/maize, Rye Vita, 100% rye bread (check the label), rice cakes, Corn Thins, rice crackers, wheat-free pasta, Pasta Regalo • Orgran baking products, teething biscuits and pasta (health shops) • Chinese rice noodles, maltabella porridge, oats porridge, Tasti Maize, popcorn, Camphill rye rusks and biscuits
Read the labels Wheat flour, semolina flour, digestive bran	**Labels** Potato flour, soya flour, rye flour, rice flour, oat flour, cornflour, spelt flour

Egg

Egg allergy occurs most commonly in children under three years of age and most outgrow it by five years of age. Both the yolk and the white can be a problem but in either case its best to avoid egg altogether as its hard to separate the egg.

Symptoms
- Skin – hives, eczema
- Asthma
- Tummy cramps, nausea, vomiting
- Hay fever
- Anaphylaxis is rare

Avoid	Replacement foods
• Albumin • Dried egg • Egg white, yolk • Egg solids, substitutes, powder • Globulin • Lecithin, Livetin, Lysozyme • Vitellin • Ovalbumin • Or anything that starts with *ovo-*	• *As a raising agent:* Substitute 5 ml/1 t of baking powder (gluten-free if necessary) for each egg in the recipe and stir in with the dry ingredients before adding any liquid. Increase the liquid content by 30 ml/2 T per egg. • *As a binder:* Dissolve 5 ml/1 t powdered gelatine in 45 ml/3 T hot water per egg. Cool, then freeze briefly until the consistency of egg white. Whisk with a fork until frothy, then use in recipe. Alternatively, when extra moisture isn't needed, use 10 ml/2 t of potato flour per egg. • *For coating:* Use 45 ml/3 T of milk (dairy-free if necessary) per beaten egg. • *To moisten a mixture,* e.g. in a rich cake: Use 50 g/¼ cup of puréed apple (apple sauce). • *To be used hard-boiled (hard-cooked) and chopped*: Use 50 g/¼ cup of crumbled, firm tofu (unless your child is allergic to soya protein). Alternatively, use the same quantity of cooked cannelloni beans, drained and roughly chopped or mashed.

Soya

Soya allergy occurs in 30% of people allergic to cows milk.

Symptoms
- Skin – hives, eczema
- Hay fever and asthma are rare
- Tummy cramps, nausea, vomiting
- Diarrhoea and intestine inflammation occurs as in dairy allergy

Avoid	Replacement foods
• Deep-fried mature soy seed, fermented soybean paste, fermented soybeans, miso, natto, soy flour, soy protein concentrates, isolates and shakes, soy sauce, soybean curds, hydrolysates, lecithin, milk, oil and sprouts, textured soy protein, textured vegetable protein (TVG), tofu, Whey-soy drink • Ingredients potentially made from soybean products • Hydrolysed plant protein • Hydrolysed soy protein • Hydrolysed vegetable protein natural flavouring • Hot dogs • Worcestershire sauce • Vegetable broth • Vegetable gum • Vegetable starch • Some breakfast cereals	To be used in cooking: • Fruit juices • Rice milk (not adequate in calcium)

Read the labels
With soya allergy the emphasis is on avoiding hidden soya in products, read labels.

References

Allergy Society of South Africa: **Information Sheets**: http://www.allergysa.org

Allergy Society of South Africa (2001): **The ALLSA Handbook of Practical Allergy 2nd Edition**

Apovian CM (2010): **The causes, prevalence, and treatment of obesity revisited in 2009: what we have learnt so far?** *The American Journal of Clinical Nutrition* 2010; 91(suppl): 277S-9S

Bhatia J, Greer F and the Committee on Nutrition (2008): **Use of Soy Protein-based Formulas in Infant Feeding.** *Pediatrics 2008*; 121: 1062-1068

Claude-Pierre P (1997): **The secret Language of Eating disorders.** Vintage Books. New York

CLINICAL GUIDELINES: PMTCT (Prevention of Mother-to-Child Transmission) 2010. National Department of Health, South Africa; South African National AIDS Council. http://www.sanac.org.za/resources/art-guidelines

Cormack B (2004): **First Foods for premature babies**. Neonatal Paediatric Dietitian. Auckland City Hospital

De Boer R, Fitzsimmon R, Brathwaite N (2009): **Eight Myths from the Food Allergy Clinic**. *Current Allergy and Clinical Immunology* 22:104-108

Deierlein AL et al (2008): **Dietary energy but no Glycaemic load is associated with gestational weight gain.** *The American Journal of Clinical Nutrition* 88:693-9

Escott-Stump S (2008): **Nutrition and Diagnosis-related Care.** Lippincott Williams & Wilkens, USA

Ferriday D, Brunstrom JM (2008): **How does food-cue exposure lead to larger meal sizes?** *British Journal of Nutrition* 100: 1325-1332

Faure M & Richardson A (2010): **Baby Sense.** Metz Press, Welgemoed

Faure M & Richardson A (2007): **Sleep Sense.** Metz Press, Welgemoed

Grant A (2007): **The baby healthy eating planner.** Bounty Books

Greer Frank R, MD; Sicherer Scott H, MD; Burks A. Wesley, MD and the Committee on Nutrition and Section on Allergy and Immunology (2007): **Effects of Early Nutritional Interventions on the Development of Atopic Disease in Infants and Children: The Role of Maternal Dietary Restriction, Breastfeeding, Timing of Introduction of Complementary Foods, and Hydrolyzed Formulas.** *Pediatrics* 121: 83-191

Gropper S, Smith S, Groff J (2009): **Advanced Nutrition and Human Metabolism.** Nelson Education LTD

Hirschmann JR & Zaphiropoulos L (1995): **Preventing Childhood Eating Problems.** Gürze Books

Hume T (2000): **Women & Food: exposing the relationship between women, food and depression.** Zebra

Kirsten GF (2009): **Does Breastfeeding Prevent Atopic Disorders?** *Current Allergy and Clinical Immunology* 22: 24 – 26

Kramer MS & Kakuma R (2002, updated in 2009): **Optimal duration of exclusive breastfeeding.** *Cochrane Database of systematic Reviews*, Issue 1. Art. No.: CD003517. DOI: 10.1002/14651858.CD003517

Koletzko B et al (2009): **Lower protein in infant formula is associated with lower weight up to age 2 y: a randomized clinical trial**. *The American Journal of Clinical Nutrition* 89:1836-45

Krebs NF and Hambidge KM (2007): **Complementary feeding: clinically relevant factors affecting timing and composition.** *The American Journal of Clinical Nutrition* 85 (suppl), 639S-645S

Lack G (2008): **Epidemiological risks for food allergy.** *Journal of allergy and clinical immunology* 121, 1331 – 1336.

LaHaye B (1997): **Understanding your child's temperament**. Harvest House Publishers

Legge B (2002): **Can't eat, won't eat – dietary difficulties and autistic spectrum disorders.** Jessica Kingsley Publishers, London and Philadelphia

Levin M, Steinman H (2009): **Mimics of Food Allergy.** *Current Allergy and Clinical Immunology* 22:110-116

Mintle L (Ph D) (2005): **Overweight Kids.** Integrity Publishers

Motala C, Hawarden D (2009): **Diagnostic testing in Allergy.** *SAMJ* 99: 531-535.

National Department of Health, South Africa; South African National AIDS Council (2010): **CLINICAL GUIDELINES: Prevention of Mother-to-Child Transmission.** http://www.sanac.org.za/resources/art-guidelines

Behrman RE, Kliegman R & Jensen HB Eds (2000): **Nelson Textbook of Pediatrics 16th edition.** WB Saunders Co

NICUS (nutrition information centre), **Feeding babies: 6 – 12 months.** www.sun.ac.za/nicus/

Olanders M (2004): **Interview with Dr Nils Bergman.** *Amningsnytt. Breastfeeding News*

Otte T (1997): **Pregnancy and Birth Book.** Struik Publishers

Potter P (2009): **Peanut Allergy in Children.** *South African Paediatric Review* 2:22-27

Potter P (2009): **Adverse Reaction to Seafood in Children: Experience in an Allergy Clinic.** *South African Paediatric Review* 2:28-34

Potter P (2009): **Inaugural Lecture Allergy in South Africa.** *Current Allergy and Clinical Immunology* 22:156-161

Prescott SL et al (2008): **The importance of early complementary feeding in the development of oral tolerance: Concerns and controversies.** *Pediatric Allergy and Immunology* 19:375-380

Rzehak P et al (2009): **Short and long term effects of feeding hydrolyzed protein infant formulas on growth at < 6 y of age: results from the German Infant Nutritional Intervention study.** *The American Journal of Clinical Nutrition* 89:1846-56.

Satter E (200): **Child of mine: feeding with love and good sense.** Bull Publishing, Palo Alto (CA)

Slaughter CW, MPH, RD; Despotopoulos AH (Bryant), MA (2004): **Hungry for Love: The Feeding Relationship in the Psychological Development of Young Children** The Permanente Journal/Winter/Volume 8 No. 1

Sowden M et al (2009): **Factors influencing high socio-economic class mothers' decision regarding formula-feeding practices in the Cape Metropole.** *South African Journal of Clinical Nutrition* 22(1)

Steinman H (2009): **Oral Allergy Syndrome – What's New.** *Current Allergy and Clinical Immunology* 22:58-62.

Sullivan K (1998): **Vitamins and Minerals – An illustrated Guide.** Element Books Limited

Van Der Poel L, Chen J, Penagos M (2009): **Food Allergy Epidemic – Is it only a Western Phenomenon.** *Current Allergy and Clinical Immunology* 22:121-126

Van der Poel L, Fox A, du Toit G (2009): **Food protein – Induced Enterocolitis Syndrome (FPEIS) – A Review.** *Current Allergy and Clinical Immunology* 22:56-57

Vickerstaff Joneja J (2007): **Dealing with food allergies in babies and children.** Bull Publishing, Colorado

Weinberg E (2010): **The Allergic March.** *SA Journal of CPD* 28:64-68

Winnicott DW (1987): **The child, the family and the outside world.** Perseus Publishing

Wolhuter T (2009): **Allergies in Infants.** *The Specialist Forum* 9:18-22

Yang Z et al (2009): **Prevalence and predictors of iron deficiency in fully breastfed infants at 6 months of age: comparison of data from 6 studies.** *The American Journal of Clinical Nutrition* 89:1433-40

Zimmerman et al (2009): **Confident commitment is a key factor for sustained breastfeeding.** Birth 36(2):141-148

Resources

BREAST-FEEDING ASSISTANCE

Lactation consultants – southafrica@iblce.edu.au

WESTERN CAPE

Lynn Shier Registered Nurse, Registered Midwife, IBCLC
Rondebosch
Tel 021-6855714 or 0833213460

Susan de Wet
Northern Suburbs
Tel 0827857770

Erica Neser
Stellenbosch
Tel 0832925252
info@babysleep.co.za

EASTERN CAPE

Dr Nan Jolly MB BCh IBCLC LLLL
Summerstrand, Port Elizabeth
Tel 0828235491
nanjolly@iafrica.com

KWA-ZULU NATAL

Claire McHugh BSc(Diet) RD
Natal
Tel 0727180567
www.childnutrition.co.za

GAUTENG

Lynda Lilienfeld RN. RM. ICEA. IBCLC.
Edenvale, Johannesburg
Tel 011-4541648 or 0827718526
baby.clinic@telkomsa.net

Sr Michelle Groom, B.Nurs (Wits), RN RM, IBCLC
Benoni
Tel 0827143330

Judy Kirkwood
Bryanston
Tel 0825621986

Michelle Gahan
Gauteng
Tel 0824532852

Hettie Grove
East Rand, Gauteng
Tel 011-8152129 or 0834925861

Katinka Fourie
Pretoria
Tel 0823760625

THE ALLERGY SOCIETY OF SOUTH AFRICA

www.allergysa.org

THE SOUTH AFRICAN PAEDIATRIC ASSOCIATION

www.paediatrician.co.za

CLEFT LIP ASSOCIATION

www.saida.org.za/societies/cleftpals

CLEFT PALS, JOHANNESBURG

Mrs Jammine
Tel 011-788 9759
listserv@home.ease.lsoft.com

CLEFT PALS, KWAZULU NATAL

Dr Pam Herber
Tel 031 8047539

CLEFT PALS: WESTERN CAPE

Mrs Ros Lentons
Speech Therapy Department, Groote Schuur
   Hospital, Cape Town
Tel 021-4046459

CLEFT PALS: FREE STATE

Rene Loftus
Tel 051-5214369

CLOTHING FOR EASY BREAST-FEEDING

Annabella maternity and beyond: www.annabellamaternity.com

POSTNATAL DEPRESSION/PERINATAL DISTRESS

PNDSA: 0828820072 www.pndsa.org.za

WEANING EQUIPMENT

Baby freezer food trays: Mumi & bubi ice trays: www.mumiandbubi.co.nz

PREM BABY RESOURCES

www.littlesteps.co.za

WEBSITES

www.babysense.co.za
www.nutripaeds.co.za

USEFUL BOOKS

Baby Sense. Megan Faure & Ann Richardson. Metz Press 2010
Sleep Sense. Megan Faure & Ann Richardson. Metz Press 2007
Toddler Sense. Ann Richardson. Metz Press, 2005
New complete baby and toddler meal planner. Annabel Karmel. Edbury, 2009
The baby healthy eating planner. Grant A. Bounty Books, 2007

ORGANIC FOODS

Ethical co-op – Cape Town: www.ethical.org.za
Bryanston organic market: www.bryanstonorganicmarket.co.za
Earth Mother – Durban: www.earthmother.co.za
Farm Shoppe – Port Elizabeth: 041-3721270

TODDLER COOKING CLASSES

Little Cooks Club nationwide: www.littlecooksclub.co.za

BABY FOOD

Healthy babe, Cape Town: www.healthybabe.com
Nutri Kidz, Cape Town: www.nutri-kidz.co.za
Pee-wee portions, Cape Town: www.peeweeportions.com
Granny's frozen baby food, Pretoria: www.grannysbabyfood.co.za

COOKING COURSES FOR MOM AND CAREGIVERS

Food for babies and toddlers: christine@littlecooksclub.co.za – Bryanston
Domestic fabulous, Cape Town: Contact Kelly: 0825745865, cookinglessons@live.co.za
Dee-lish cooking, Durban: www.deelishdbn.wordpress.com
Domestic cooking classes nationwide: www.eat-in.co.za

BABY SIGNING

Baby Hands SA: www.babyhands.co.za

NANNY TRAINING

Sugar and Spice Nanny Training: www.nannytraining.co.za
Nanny Training: www.momsbabiesnannies.co.za

BABIES WITH SPECIAL NEEDS

Special kids magazine: Nina – blackinc@mweb.co.za
Special kids therapy centre – Cape Town: www.animakids.co.za
Breast-feeding your special needs baby: www.llli.org/FAQ/disabled
Resource website for babies with special needs: www.comeunity.com

Index

Other books in the series

Baby Sense by Megan Faure and Ann Richardson
This best selling baby care book in South Africa, has been translated into several languages and has twice won a prestigious international award (UK Practical Pre-school Awards Gold in 2008 and 2009). Now fully updated, the book's accessible tone and the focus on baby's sleep, calming and development remain in the new edition which reflects current research, and addresses questions and requests from both moms and professionals.

The new edition is sure to hold the same appeal for parents in that it offers practical solutions for the common issues of infancy. The new content will enhance the ways parents respond to their baby's sensory needs in a sense-able manner.

Sleep Sense by Megan Faure and Ann Richardson
Simple, sensible solutions to ensure you and your baby will get a good night's sleep by establishing healthy sleeping habits. Learn to set the stage for sleep with
- realistic expectations
- appropriate sensory experiences during the day
- the right sleep zone
- the elimination of hunger or medical reasons for night wakings
- healthy and sufficient day sleeps
- good sleep associations to prime your baby for independent night soothing
- solutions for separation issues.

An an age-related trouble shooting section offers desperate parents quick fixes based on the natural and age-appropriate capacity their baby has for self-calming or soothing, and for separation from them.

Toddler Sense by Ann Richardson
Toddlerhood is a time of tremendous growth and development. It is also a time of tantrums and conflict. Knowing what constitutes normal toddler behaviour will help you accept and respect this and go a long way towards effective, guilt-free and realistic parenting. Your toddler learns though his senses – understanding his sensory world remains the key to ensuring optimal development and stimulation. This book tells you how to
- Provide stimulation without overload
- Solve bedtime battles with age-appropriate sleep-training
- Discipline with love and a sense of humour
- Follow a sensible approach to toilet training
- Monitor and encourage development
- Deal with feeding issues without stress.